BEGINNING JAPANESE PHRASES

WRITING PRACTICE PAD

WILLIAM MATSUZAKI

TUTTLE Publishing

Tokyo | Rutland, Vermont | Singapore

Published by Tuttle Publishing, an imprint of Periplus Editions (HK) Ltd.

www.tuttlepublishing.com

ISBN 978-0-8048-5520-4

Distributed by

North America, Latin America & Europe
Tuttle Publishing
364 Innovation Drive, North Clarendon
VT 05759-9436 U.S.A.
Tel: 1 (802) 773-8930
Fax: 1 (802) 773-6993
info@tuttlepublishing.com
www.tuttlepublishing.com

Japan
Tuttle Publishing
Yaekari Building, 3rd Floor, 5-4-12 Osaki
Shinagawa-ku, Tokyo 141 0032
Tel: (81) 3 5437-0171
Fax: (81) 3 5437-0755
sales@tuttle.co.jp
www.tuttle.co.jp

Asia Pacific
Berkeley Books Pte. Ltd.
3 Kallang Sector #04-01, Singapore 349278
Tel: (65) 6741-2178
Fax: (65) 6741-2179
inquiries@periplus.com.sg
www.tuttlepublishing.com

"Books to Span the East and West"

Tuttle Publishing was founded in 1832 in the small New England town of Rutland, Vermont [USA]. Our core values remain as strong today as they were then—to publish best-in-class books which bring people together one page at a time. In 1948, we established a publishing office in Japan—and Tuttle is now a leader in publishing English-language books about the arts, languages and cultures of Asia. The world has become a much smaller place today and Asia's economic and cultural influence has grown. Yet the need for meaningful dialogue and information about this diverse region has never been greater. Over the past seven decades, Tuttle has published thousands of books on subjects ranging from martial arts and paper crafts to language learning and literature—and our talented authors, illustrators, designers and photographers have won many prestigious awards. We welcome you to explore the wealth of information available on Asia at **www.tuttlepublishing.com**.

First edition
26 25 24 23 22
10 9 8 7 6 5 4 3 2 1 2201EP

Printed in China

INTRODUCTION

Welcome to *Beginning Japanese Phrases Writing Practice Pad*—it is the perfect tool to start your study in Japanese. Five minutes a day is all you need—and you're on your way to speaking and writing Japanese!

Each sheet in this pad introduces a new Japanese phrase in bold, easy-to-read type, with the pronunciation and meaning in English. Grammar Notes are provided along with Etiquette Tips on when and how to use the phrase. Practice spaces are provided so you can write the phrase while memorizing it, and exercises are given on the back.

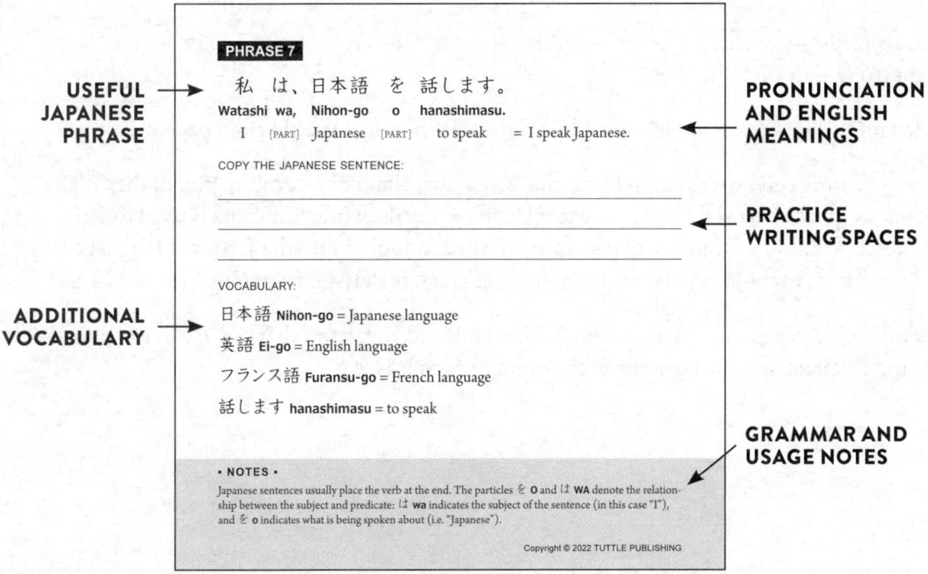

PHRASE 7

私　は、日本語　を　話します。

Watashi wa, Nihon-go o hanashimasu.

I [PART] Japanese [PART] to speak = I speak Japanese.

COPY THE JAPANESE SENTENCE:

VOCABULARY:

日本語 **Nihon-go** = Japanese language

英語 **Ei-go** = English language

フランス語 **Furansu-go** = French language

話します **hanashimasu** = to speak

• NOTES •

Japanese sentences usually place the verb at the end. The particles を **O** and は **WA** denote the relationship between the subject and predicate: は **wa** indicates the subject of the sentence (in this case "I"), and を **o** indicates what is being spoken about (i.e. "Japanese").

Copyright © 2022 TUTTLE PUBLISHING

PRONUNCIATION

Japanese sounds are relatively easy to pronounce and they do not have tones, unlike many Asian languages. The basic vowels (A, I, U, E, O) are pronounced:

A sounds like the **a** in "ah"
I sounds like the **e** in "eat"
U sounds like the **oo** in "shoo"
E sounds like the **eh** in "best"
O sounds like the **o** in "ok"

Some Japanese sounds have vowels that are pronounced twice as long, shown by a macron over the vowel in the Romanized form, e.g.:

dōzo (= please, go ahead)
intānetto (= Internet, the Web)

All Japanese consonants are followed by a vowel, as shown in the chart on page v.

Japanese words can be written in Hiragana, Katakana, Kanji or a combination of these. The Hiragana alphabet is used mainly to write Japanese words, while Katakana is used to write loanwords from other sources, that is, foreign words adopted into the Japanese language (e.g マネージャー **manējā** "manager"). Kanji are characters derived from Chinese.

The following pages show the combined Hiragana and Katakana chart. Hiragana is given on the left, and Katakana on the right for each sound in each box, e.g.:

が ガ **GA**

HIRAGANA AND KATAKANA CHART

	A	I	U	E	O	Combined Sounds		
Single sound	あア A	いイ I	うウ U	えエ E	おオ O			
K	かカ KA	きキ KI	くク KU	けケ KE	こコ KO	きゃキャ KYA	きゅキュ KYU	きょキョ KYO
S	さサ SA	しシ SHI	すス SU	せセ SE	そソ SO	しゃシャ SHA	しゅシュ SHU	しょショ SHO
T	たタ TA	ちチ CHI	つツ TSU	てテ TE	とト TO	ちゃチャ CHA	ちゅチュ CHU	ちょチョ CHO
N	なナ NA	にニ NI	ぬヌ NU	ねネ NE	のノ NO	にゃニャ NYA	にゅニュ NYU	にょニョ NYO
H	はハ HA	ひヒ HI	ふフ FU	へヘ HE	ほホ HO	ひゃヒャ HYA	ひゅヒュ HYU	ひょヒョ HYO
M	まマ MA	みミ MI	むム MU	めメ ME	もモ MO	みゃミャ MYA	みゅミュ MYU	みょミョ MYO
Y	やヤ YA		ゆユ YU		よヨ YO			
R	らラ RA	りリ RI	るル RU	れレ RE	ろロ RO	りゃリャ RYA	りゅリュ RYU	りょリョ RYO
W	わワ WA		んン N		をヲ O			
G	がガ GA	ぎギ GI	ぐグ GU	げゲ GE	ごゴ GO	ぎゃギャ GYA	ぎゅギュ GYU	ぎょギョ GYO
Z	ざザ ZA	じジ JI	ずズ ZU	ぜゼ ZE	ぞゾ ZO	じゃジャ JA	じゅジュ JU	じょジョ JO

HIRAGANA AND KATAKANA CHART (continued)

	A	I	U	E	O	Combined Sounds		
D	だダ **DA**	ぢヂ **JI**	づヅ **ZU**	でデ **DE**	どド **DO**	ぢゃヂャ **JA**	ぢゅヂュ **JU**	ぢょヂョ **JO**
B	ばバ **BA**	びビ **BI**	ぶブ **BU**	べベ **BE**	ぼボ **BO**	びゃビャ **BYA**	びゅビュ **BYU**	びょビョ **BYO**
P	ぱパ **PA**	ぴピ **PI**	ぷプ **PU**	ぺペ **PE**	ぽポ **PO**	ぴゃピャ **PYA**	ぴゅピュ **PYU**	ぴょピョ **PYO**

JAPANESE PARTICLES

Like English prepositions and conjunctions, Japanese particles play an important role in sentences. They indicate the relationship between different components in a sentence. The following are some common Japanese particles:

は **wa**	denotes a sentence topic
を **o**	used after a direct object
か **ka**	signifies a question
に **ni**	*in*; *at*; used after a location or time word
の **no**	possession; replaces a noun
が **ga**	new information marker; *but*; conjunction; used to combine two sentences
も **mo**	*too*; *also*; replaces particles は, が, and を

と **to**	used like English *and* when connecting two or more nouns; quotation particle used after quotation
から **kara**	*from* (a place or a time); *from* (used with specific times or locations)
へ/に **e/ni**	used with verbs of movement
まで **made**	*until* (used with specific locations or times)
でも **demo**	*but* or *however* (used at the beginning of a sentence)

ね **ne**	sentence ending for a rhetorical question or when seeking agreement
ねえ **nē**	sentence ending that can be exclamatory or expresses surprise
よ **yo**	sentence ending for a strong declarative statement or for emphasis

で **de**	by means of a "tool"; comes after the place of action; *for* (used for shopping or ordering food)
など **nado**	etcetera, and so forth

JAPANESE VERBS

Unlike most languages, Japanese verbs do not depend on whether the subject is singular or plural, male or female, first person or second person, etc. They are placed at the end of sentences, and the various forms of verbs give details of a speaker's intention, mood or expectation, etc.

Japanese verbs can be classified into three groups: Group 1, Group 2 and Group 3. Some common examples of each group of verbs are as follows:

<u>Group 1 (most **I**-ending verbs)</u>

買います **kai-masu** ("to buy")
書きます **kaki-masu** ("to write")
飲みます **nomi-masu** ("to drink")
あります **ari-masu** ("to exist/have")

<u>Group 2 (all **E**-ending verbs and some I-ending verbs)</u>

食べます **tabe-masu** ("to eat")
見ます **mi-masu** ("to see")

<u>Group 3 (the irregular verbs)</u>

します **shimasu** ("to do")
来ます **kimasu** ("to come")

All three groups of verbs can exhibit many forms.

Tables Showing the Various Verb Forms for Each Group

Group	Eng. meaning	masu form ます	Dictionary form	Negtive form -nai ない	Gerund -te form て	Tentative -yō form よう	Provisional -ba form ば
Group 1	to buy	買います **kai-masu**	買う **ka-u**	買わない **kawa-nai**	買って **kat-te**	買おう **ka-ō**	買えば **kae-ba**
	to write	書きます **kaki-masu**	書く **ka-ku**	書かない **kaka-nai**	書いて **kai-te**	書こう **ka-kō**	書けば **kake-ba**
	to drink	飲みます **nomi-masu**	飲む **no-mu**	飲まない **noma-nai**	飲んで **non-de**	飲もう **no-mō**	飲めば **nome-ba**
	to exist	あります **ari-masu**	ある **a-ru**	ない **nai**	あって **at-te**	あろう **a-rō**	あれば **are-ba**
Group 2	to eat	食べます **tabe-masu**	食べる **tabe-ru**	食べない **tabe-nai**	食べて **tabe-te**	食べよう **tabe-yō**	食べれば **tabe-reba**
	to see	見ます **mi-masu**	見る **mi-ru**	見ない **mi-nai**	見て **mi-te**	見よう **mi-yō**	見れば **mi-reba**
Group 3	to do	します **shi-masu**	する **su-ru**	しない **shi-nai**	して **shi-te**	しよう **shi-yō**	すれば **su-reba**
	to come	来ます **ki-masu**	来る **ku-ru**	来ない **ko-nai**	来て **ki-te**	来よう **ko-yō**	来れば **ku-reba**

Notes

1. The -**MASU** form of verb is usually referred to as the "polite form." It is used in normal speaking when one needs to be polite.
2. The dictionary form, also known as the plain form, is used when one is in the company of friends, family and other close associates.
3. The **TE** form—this can be used to form nouns in Japanese. It is converted from the dictionary form:

a) Group 1 verbs:
Change the ending from the "e" line of the Kana chart

-ku → -ite	書く **ka-ku**	→	書いて **ka-ite**
-gu → -ide	脱ぐ **nu-gu**	→	脱いで **nu-ide**
-su → -shite	貸す **ka-su**	→	貸して **ka-shite**
-bu	運ぶ **hako-bu**	→	運んで **hako-nde**
-mu → -nde	飲む **no-mu**	→	飲んで **no-nde**
-nu	死ぬ **shi-nu**	→	死んで **shi-nde**
-ru → -itte	切る **ki-ru**	→	切って **ki-tte**
-tsu → -tte	立つ **ta-tsu**	→	立って **ta-tte**
-u → -tte	会う **a-u**	→	会って **a-tte**

(if preceded by vowel)

b) Group 2 verbs:

-ru → -te
食べる **tabe-ru** → 食べて **tabe-te**
見る **mi-ru** → 見て **mi-te**

b) Group 3 verbs:

suru → -shite する **su-ru** → して **shi-te**
kuru → kite 来る **ku-ru** → 来て **ki-te**

The **te** form + **kudasai** is used in polite requests, e.g.
書いてください **ka-ite kudasai** (Please write.)
食べてください **tabe-te kudasai** (Please eat.)
来てください **ki-te kudasai** (Please come.)

4. The **shō** form (Let's …)
Attaching **shō** to the root stem* of a verb gives an invitation to do something together:
食べましょうか。**Tabemashō ka.** (Let's eat, shall we?)

*This is the verb in the **-MASU** form after the "**su**" has been dropped off.

HOW TO COUNT IN JAPANESE

0 れい/ゼロ **rei; zero**

1 いち **ichi**

2 に **ni**

3 さん **san**

4 よん **yon**/し **shi**

5 ご **go**

6 ろく **roku**

7 しち **shiich**/なな **nana**

8 はち **hachi**

9 きゅう **kyū**/く **ku**

10 じゅう **jū**

11 じゅういち **jū ichi**

12 じゅうに **jū ni**

13 じゅうさん **jū san**

14 じゅうよん **jū yon**/
じゅうし **jū shi**

15 じゅうご **jū go**

16 じゅうろく **jū roku**

17 じゅうしち **jū shichi**/
じゅうなな **jū nana**

18 じゅうはち **jū hachi**

19 じゅうきゅう **jū kyū**/
じゅうく **jū ku**

20 にじゅう **nijū**

30 さんじゅう **sanjū**

40 よんじゅう **yonjū**

50 ごじゅう **gojū**

60 ろくじゅう **rokujū**

70 ななじゅう **nanajū**

80 はちじゅう **hachijū**

90 きゅうじゅう **kyūjū**

100 ひゃく **hyaku**

200 にひゃく **nihyaku**

300 さんびゃく **sanbyaku**

400 よんひゃく **yonhyaku**

500 ごひゃく **gohyaku**

600 ろっぴゃく **roppyaku**

700 ななひゃく **nanahyaku**

800 はっぴゃく **happyaku**

900 きゅうひゃく **kyūhyaku**

1,000 せん **sen**

2,000 にせん **nisen**

3,000 さんぜん **sanzen**

4,000 よんせん **yonsen**

5,000 ごせん **gosen**

6,000 ろくせん **rokusen**

7,000 ななせん **nanasen**

8,000 はっせん **hassen**

9,000 きゅうせん **kyūsen**

10,000 いちまん **ichiman**

Common Counters

	個 **-ko** piece	才 **-sai** years old	-杯 **-hai** cupfuls		個 **-ko** piece	才 **-sai** years old	-杯 **-hai** cupfuls
1	**ik-ko**	**is-sai**	**ip-pai**	6	**rok-ko**	**rok-sai**	**rop-pai**
2	**ni-ko**	**ni-sai**	**ni-hai**	7	**nana-ko**	**nana-sai**	**nana-hai**
3	**san-ko**	**san-sai**	**san-bai**	8	**hachi-ko, hak-ko**	**has-sai**	**hap-pai**
4	**yon-ko**	**yon-sai**	**yon-hai**				
5	**go-ko**	**go-sai**	**go-hai**	9	**kyū-ko**	**kyū-sai**	**kyū-hai**

	個 **-ko** piece	才 **-sai** years old	-杯 **-hai** cupfuls		個 **-ko** piece	才 **-sai** years old	-杯 **-hai** cupfuls
10	**juk-ko, jik-ko**	**jus-sai, jis-sai**	**jup-pai**	How ...?	**nan-ko**	**nan-sai**	**nan-bai**

The other common counters:

- -枚 **-mai** flat, thin objects (sheets, dishes, newspapers, etc.)
- -本 **-hon** slender objects (pencils, sticks, bottles, flowers, etc.)
- -冊 **-satsu** (bound) volumes (books, magazines, etc.)
- -通 **-tsū** letters
- -頭 **-tō** large animals (horses, cows, etc.)
- -匹 **-hiki** animals, fish, insects
- -羽 **-wa** animals, birds, rabbits
- -着 **-chaku** suits, dresses
- -ページ **-pēji** page ... (e.g. 2 pages of text)

Secondary Counters

	つ **-tsu** numerals	人 **-nin** people	-箱 **-hako** boxfuls		つ **-tsu** numerals	人 **-nin** people	-箱 **-hako** boxfuls
1	**hitotsu**	**hitori**	**hito-hako**	7	**nanatsu**	**nana-nin, shichi-nin**	**nana-hako**
2	**futatsu**	**futari**	**futa-hako**				
3	**mittsu**	**san-nin**	**san-pako**	8	**yattsu**	**hachi-nin**	**hap-pako**
4	**yottsu**	**yo-nin**	**yon-hako**	9	**kokonotsu**	**kyū-nin**	**kyū-hako**
5	**itsutsu**	**go-nin**	**go-hako**	10	**tō**	**jū-nin**	**jūp-pako**
6	**muttsu**	**roku-nin**	**rop-pako**	How ...?	**ikutsu**	**nan-nin**	**nan-hako**

The other secondary counters:

- -晩 **-ban** nights
- -袋 **-fukuro** bagfuls
- -間 **-ma** rooms
- -切れ **-kire** slices, cuts, pieces
- -組 **-kumi** groups, sets (of matched objects)
- -皿 **-sara** platefuls
- -束 **-taba** bunches

Counting Time and Periods of Time

	時 -ji o'clock	時間 -jikan hour	分 -fun minute	週間 -shūkan week	ヶ月 -kagetsu month	年 -nen year
1	ichi-ji	ichi-jikan	ip-pun	is-shūkan	ik-kagetsu	ichi-nen
2	ni-ji	ni-jikan	ni-fun	ni-shūkan	ni-kagetsu	ni-nen
3	san-ji	san-jikan	san-pun	san-shūkan	san-kagetsu	san-nen
4	yo-ji	yo-jikan	yon-pun	yon-shūkan	yon-kagetsu	yo-nen
5	go-ji	go-jikan	go-fun	go-shūkan	go-kagetsu	go-nen
6	roku-ji	roku-jikan	rop-pun	roku-shūkan	rok-kagetsu	roku-nen
7	nana-ji	nana-jikan, shichi-jikan	nana-fun	nana-shūkan	nana-kagetsu	nana-nen, shichi-nen
8	hachi-ji	hachi-jikan	hap-pun	has-shūkan	hak-kagetsu	hachi-nen
9	ku-ji	ku-jikan	kyū-fun	kyū-shūkan	kyū-kagetsu	kyū-nen
10	jū-ji	jū-jikan	jup-pun, jip-pun	jus-shūkan	juk-kagetsu	jū-nen
11	jū ichi-ji	jū ichi-jikan	jū ip-pun	jū is-shūkan	jū ik-kagetsu	jū ichi-nen
12	jū ni-ji	jū ni-jikan	jū ni-fun	jū ni-shūkan	jū ni-kagetsu	jū ni-nen
How ...?	nan-ji	nan-jikan	nan-pun	nan-shūkan	nan-kagetsu	nan-nen

Counting Days

1日	**tsuitachi**	9日	**kokonoka**	17日	**jūshichi-nichi**	25日	**nijū go-nichi**
2日	**futsuka**	10日	**tōka**	18日	**jūhachi-nichi**	26日	**nijū roku-nichi**
3日	**mikka**	11日	**jūichi-nichi**	19日	**jūku-nichi**	27日	**nijū shichi-nichi**
4日	**yokka**	12日	**jūni-nichi**	20日	**hatsuka**	28日	**nijū hachi-nichi**
5日	**itsuka**	13日	**jūsan-nichi**	21日	**nijū ichi-nichi**	29日	**nijū ku-nichi**
6日	**muika**	14日	**jūyokka**	22日	**nijū ni-nichi**	30日	**sanjū-nichi**
7日	**nanoka**	15日	**jūgo-nichi**	23日	**nijū san-nichi**	31日	**sanjū ichi-nichi**
8日	**yōka**	16日	**jūroku-nichi**	24日	**nijū yokka**		

Some Useful Vocabulary

A) Festivals and events in Japan

1月1日
1 January
元旦 **gantan**, 元日 **ganjitsu**
New Year's Day

1月第2月曜日
2nd Mon. of Jan.
成人の日 **Seijin no hi**
Coming-of-Age Day

2月4日
4 February
節分 **Setsubun**
The close of Winter Festival

2月11日
11 February
建国記念の日
Kenkoku Kinen no hi
National Foundation Day

2月23日
23 February
天皇誕生日 **Tennō Tanjōbi**
Emperor's Birthday

3月3日
3 March
ひな祭り **Hinamatsuri**
Girls' Festival

3月21日
Around 21 March
春分の日 **Shunbun no hi**
Vernal Equinox Day

4月29日
29 April
昭和の日 **Shōwa no hi**
Showa Day

5月3日
3 May
憲法記念日 **Kenpō Kinenbi**
Constitution Day

5月4日
4 May
みどりの日 **Midori no hi**
Greenery Day

5月5日 *5 May*	子供の日 **Kodomo no hi** Children's Day
7月第3月曜日 *3rd Mon. of July*	海の日 **Umi no hi** Marine Day
8月11日 *11 August*	山の日 **Yama no hi** Mountain Day
9月第3月曜日 *3rd Monday of September*	敬老の日 **Keirō no hi** Respect-for-Aged Day
9月23日 *23 September*	秋分の日 **Shūbun no hi** Autumnal Equinox Day
10月第2月曜日 *2nd Monday of October*	体育の日 **Taiiku no hi** Sports Day
11月3日 *3 November*	文化の日 **Bunka no hi** Culture Day
11月23日 *23 November*	勤労感謝の日 **Kinro Kansha no hi** Labor Thanksgiving Day

b) Common Food in Japan

肉/魚 **niku/sakana** meat/fish	果物 **kudamono** fruit
牛肉 **gyūniku** beef 鶏肉 **toriniku** chicken (meat) 豚肉 **butaniku** pork ひき肉 **hikiniku** minced meat 魚 **sakana** fish うなぎ **unagi** Japanese eel	みかん **mikan** tangerine りんご **ringo** apple いちご **ichigo** strawberry バナナ **banana** banana ぶどう **budō** grape もも **momo** peach なし **nashi** pear

定番の食べ物 **teiban no tabemono** everyday food	
味噌 **miso** bean paste, miso しょうゆ **shōyu** soy sauce 砂糖 **satō** sugar 塩 **shio** salt 油 **abura** cooking oil	お茶 **o-cha** green tea 紅茶 **kōcha** black tea 酒 **sake** Japanese rice wine, saké 牛乳 **gyūnyū** milk

野菜 **yasai** vegetables
きゅうり **kyūri** cucumber 長ねぎ **naga-negi** scallion, green onion 玉ねぎ **tamanegi** onion ほうれん草 **hōrensō** spinach じゃがいも **jagaimo** potato にんじん **ninjin** carrot だいこん **daikon** radish 枝豆 **edamame** edamame レタス **retasu** lettuce トマト **tomato** tomato ピーマン **pīman** bell pepper キャベツ **kyabetsu** cabbage ごぼう **gobō** burdock root

定番の食べ物 **teiban no tabemono** everyday food		
米 **kome** uncooked rice ごはん **gohan** (cooked) rice 豆腐 **tōfu** tofu, bean curd なっとう **nattō** *natto,* fermented soy bean 卵 **tamago** egg 餅 **mochi** rice cake 梅干し **umeboshi** pickled plum 漬け物 **tsukemono** pickles 味噌汁 **misoshiru** miso soup そば **soba** buckwheat noodle うどん **udon** wheat noodle	和食 **washoku** Japanese-style food 牛丼 **gyū-don** beef-over-rice-bowl 天丼 **ten-don** bowl of rice with tenpura かつ丼 **katsu-don** bowl of rice with pork cutlet おにぎり **onigiri** rice ball とんかつ **tonkatsu** pork cutlet 天ぷら **tenpura** tenpura 刺身 **sashimi** sashimi	お弁当 **o-bentō** box lunch お寿司 **o-sushi** sushi 焼き鳥 **yakitori** grilled chicken 洋食 **yōshoku** Western-style food カレーライス **karē-raisu** curry and rice ハンバーガー **hanbāgā** hamburger 中華料理 **chūkaryōri** Chinese-style food ラーメン **rāmen** ramen

c) Useful phrases to use when traveling, shopping, etc

すみません。
Sumimaen.
Excuse me.

ちょっといいですか。
Chotto ii desu ka.
May I ask you something?

どうもありがとう。
Domō arigatō.
Thank you.

on the phone
もしもし。
Moshi-moshi.
Hello?

sales clerk → customer
いらっしゃいませ。
Irasshaimase.
Hello! May I help you?

sales clerk → customer
ありがとうございました。
Arigatō gozaimashita.
Thank you for coming/calling.

大丈夫です。
Daijōbu desu.
I'm okay.

大丈夫ですよ。
Daijōbu desu yo.
That's all right.

大丈夫ですか。
Daijōbu desu ka.
Are you okay now?

Sample Phrases The underlined can be replaced by other words as given below.

Sample sentence 1 ⟶

駅はどこですか。
Eki wa doko desu ka.
Where is the train station?

この場所へ行きたいんですが。
Kono basho e ikitai n desu ga.
I want to go to this place.

Vocabulary A

病院 **byōin** hospital
薬局 **yakkyoku** pharmacy
空港 **kūkō** airport
バス停 **basutei** bus stop
トイレ **toire** bathroom
案内所 **an'naisho** (tourist) information center
デパート **depāto** department store
スーパー **sūpā** supermarket
お寺 **otera** temple
神社 **jinja** shrine

Sample sentence 2 ⟶

チェックインしたいんですが。
Chekku-in shitai n desu ga.
I want to check in.

Vocabulary B

チェックアウトする **chekku-auto suru** check out
両替する **ryōgae suru** to exchange money
予約する **yoyaku suru** to make a reservation
充電する **jūden suru** to recharge the battery

Sample sentence 3 ⟶

これをください。
Kore o kudasai.
I will have this one.

これはいくらですか。
Kore wa ikura desu ka.
How much is this?

Vocabulary C

ビール **bīru** beer
ワイン **wain** wine
コーラ **kōra** coke
お茶 **ocha** green tea
オレンジジュース **orenji jūsu** orange juice
たばこ **tabako** cigarette
扇子 **sensu** fan
着物 **kimono** Japanese kimono

Sample sentence 4 ⟶

財布をなくしました。
Saifu o nakushimashita
I lost my wallet.

Vocabulary D

パスポート **pasupōto** passport
切符 **kippu** ticket
手荷物 **tenimotsu** luggage
スマホ **sumaho** smart-phone

PHRASE 1

おはよう ございます。

Ohayō **gozaimasu.**

Early there is = Good morning.

COPY THE JAPANESE SENTENCE:

VOCABULARY:

こんにちは。**Konnichiwa.** = Good afternoon.

こんばんは。**Konbanwa.** = Good evening.

おやすみなさい。**Oyasuminasai.** = Good night.

ございます。**gozaimasu** = there is

▪ NOTES ▪

ございます **gozaimasu** is the polite form of あります **arimasu**. In Japanese, there are two words for "there is." If the subject of the sentence is animate, such as an animal or a person, you use the word います **imasu**. However, if the subject is inanimate, such as a chair or a cup, you use the word あります **arimasu**.

WRITE THE FOLLOWING IN JAPANESE:

1. Good afternoon.

2. Good evening.

3. Good night.

1. こんにちは。
2. こんばんは。
3. おやすみなさい。

PHRASE 2

はじめ　まして。

Hajime mashite.

First (time) met [PAST TENSE] = How do you do?

COPY THE JAPANESE SENTENCE:

VOCABULARY:

おげんきですか。**Ogenki desu ka.** = How are you?

お会いできてうれしいです。

Oaidekite ureshii desu. = Nice to meet you.

おげんきで **Ogenki de.** = Good luck.

▪ NOTES ▪

おげんきですか **Ogenki desu ka.** It is often translated into "How are you", but it's not used on the people you meet every day like English "How are you?", but on the people you meet after a long time.

WRITE THE FOLLOWING IN JAPANESE:

1. How are you?

____

____

2. Nice to meet you.

____

____

3. Good luck.

____

____

1. おげんきですか。
2. お会いできてうれしいです。
3. おげんきで。

PHRASE 3

さようなら。

Sayōnara.

Good-bye.

COPY THE JAPANESE SENTENCE:

VOCABULARY:

じゃあ　また。**Jā mata.** = See you.

じゃあね。**Jā ne.** = Bye.

また　あした。**Mata ashita.** = See you tomorrow.

▪ NOTES ▪

さようなら **Sayōnara** — This literally means "definitely." Said by the person leaving. じゃあね **Jā ne** is the colloquial form of さようなら **Sayōnara**.

WRITE THE FOLLOWING IN JAPANESE:

1. See you.

2. Bye.

3. See you tomorrow.

1. じゃあまた。
2. じゃあね。
3. またあした。

PHRASE 4

いって　きます。

Itte　　kimasu.

To go　to come back　= I'm going now.

COPY THE JAPANESE SENTENCE:

VOCABULARY:

いってらっしゃい！ **Itterasshai!** = Have a nice trip!

ただいま！ **Tadaima!** = I'm home!

おかえりなさい！ **Okaerinasai!** = Welcome back!

▪ NOTES ▪

いってきます **Itte kimasu** is said by the one going out, while いってらっしゃい **Itterasshai** is a response to this greeting. ただいま **Tadaima** is said by the one returning home or to the office, while おかえりなさい **Okaerinasai** is a response to this greeting.

WRITE THE FOLLOWING IN JAPANESE:

1. Have a nice trip!

____

____

2. I'm home!

____

____

3. Welcome back!

____

____

1. いってらっしゃい。
2. ただいま。
3. おかえりなさい。

PHRASE 5

どうぞ　よろしく　おねがい　します。

Dōzo	**yoroshiku**	**onegai**	**shimasu.**
Please	thank	wish	to do

= It will be much appreciated.

COPY THE JAPANESE SENTENCE:

___

___

___

VOCABULARY:

ごめんなさい。**Gomen'nasai** = I'm sorry.

すみません。**Sumimasen** = Excuse me.

おめでとう　ございます。**Omedetō gozaimasu.** = Congratulations!

▪ NOTES ▪

ごめんなさい **Gomen'nasai** is a casual expression of an apology. In daily conversation, すいません **Suimasen** is overwhelmingly used and can also be used as a light apology. The polite form is すみません **Sumimasen**.

WRITE THE FOLLOWING IN JAPANESE:

1. I'm sorry.

2. Excuse me.

3. Congratulations!

1. ごめんなさい。
2. すみません。
3. おめでとうございます。

PHRASE 6

おさき に しつれい します。

Osaki ni shitsurei shimasu.

Early [PART] sorry to do

= Excuse me for leaving (before you).

COPY THE JAPANESE SENTENCE:

VOCABULARY:

おつかれさまでした。**Otsukaresama deshita.**
= Thank you for the hard work.

がんばって！ **Ganbatte!** = Go for it!

きを つけて！ **Ki o tsukete!** = Take care!

▪ NOTES ▪

おさきにしつれいします **Osaki ni shitsurei shimasu**, said when you leave office earlier than others. (Lit. I'm sorry to leave early.) おつかれさまでした **Otsukaresama deshita** is a reply to おさきにしつれいします **Osaki ni shitsurei shimasu.** きをつけて **ki o tsukete is said** to the person who will go on a trip.

WRITE THE FOLLOWING IN JAPANESE:

1. Thank you for the hard work.

2. Go for it!

3. Take care!

1. おつかれさまでした。
2. がんばって。
3. きをつけて。

PHRASE 7

私　は、日本語　を　話します。

Watashi　wa,　Nihon-go　o　hanashimasu.

I [PART] Japanese [PART] to speak = I speak Japanese.

COPY THE JAPANESE SENTENCE:

VOCABULARY:

日本語 **Nihon-go** = Japanese language

英語 **Ei-go** = English language

フランス語 **Furansu-go** = French language

話します **hanashimasu** = to speak

▪ **NOTES** ▪

Japanese sentences usually place the verb at the end. The particles を **O** and は **WA** denote the relationship between the subject and predicate: は **wa** indicates the subject of the sentence (in this case "I"), and を **o** indicates what is being spoken about (i.e. "Japanese").

WRITE THE FOLLOWING IN JAPANESE:

1. I speak Japanese.

2. I speak French.

3. I speak English.

1. 私は、日本語を話します。
2. 私は、フランス語を話します。
3. 私は、英語を話します。

PHRASE 8

私　は、中国　で　生まれました。

Watashi wa, Chūgoku de umaremashita.

I [PART] China [PART] was born = I was born in China.

COPY THE JAPANESE SENTENCE:

VOCABULARY:

日本 **Nihon** = Japan

アメリカ **Amerika** = U.S.

中国 **Chūgoku** = China

生まれました **umaremashita** = was born in

▪ NOTES ▪

The particle で **DE** is usually translated as “at” or “in” with the pattern of PLACE and ACTION VERB.

WRITE THE FOLLOWING IN JAPANESE:

1. I was born in China.

2. I was born in Japan.

3. I was born in the U.S.

1. 私は、中国で生まれました。
2. 私は、日本で生まれました。
3. 私は、アメリカで生まれました。

PHRASE 9

これ は、 紙 です。

Kore wa, kami desu.

This [PART] paper [COPULA] = This is paper.

COPY THE JAPANESE SENTENCE:

VOCABULARY:

これ **kore** = this

紙 **kami** = paper

ごみばこ **gomibako** = trash can

ラップトップ **rapputoppu** = laptop

▪ NOTES ▪

In this sentence structure, you see です **DESU**. This is called the copula, which is used at the end of the sentence right after an adjective or a noun.

WRITE THE FOLLOWING IN JAPANESE:

1. This is a laptop.

2. This is a trash can.

3. This is paper.

1. これは、ラップトップです。
2. これは、ごみばこです。
3. これは、紙です。

PHRASE 10

それ は、ピザ です。

Sore wa, piza desu.

That [PART] pizza [COPULA] = That is pizza.

COPY THE JAPANESE SENTENCE:

VOCABULARY:

それ **sore** = that

ピザ **piza** = pizza

草 **kusa** = grass

ステーキ **sutēki** = steak

▪ NOTES ▪

Similar to English, これ **KORE** is used when the object is closer to the speaker, and それ **SORE** when the object is closer to the listener.

WRITE THE FOLLOWING IN JAPANESE:

1. That is steak.

2. That is grass.

3. That is paper.

1. それは、ステーキです。
2. それは、草です。
3. それは、紙です。

PHRASE 11

あれ　は、まんが　です。

Are　wa,　manga　desu.

That over there [PART] comics [COPULA] = That over there is a comic.

COPY THE JAPANESE SENTENCE:

VOCABULARY:

あれ **are** = that over there

まんが **manga** = comics

タクシー **takushī** = taxi

船 **fune** = boat

▪ NOTES ▪

あれ **ARE** is used when the object is far from both the speaker and the listener.

WRITE THE FOLLOWING IN JAPANESE:

1. That over there is a boat.

2. That over there is a taxi.

3. That over there is a comic.

1. あれは、船です。
2. あれは、タクシーです。
3. あれは、まんがです。

PHRASE 12

私　は、赤　が　好き　です。

Watashi wa, aka ga suki desu.

I [PART] red [PART] like [COPULA] = I like red.

COPY THE JAPANESE SENTENCE:

VOCABULARY:

赤 **aka** = red

好き **suki** = like

青 **ao** = blue

黒 **kuro** = black

▪ NOTES ▪

In Japanese, all formal verbs end in ます **MASU**. When a formal sentence does not end with a verb, it ends with a です **DESU**, which is a copula.

WRITE THE FOLLOWING IN JAPANESE:

1. I like red.

2. I like blue.

3. I like black.

1. 私は、赤が好きです。
2. 私は、青が好きです。
3. 私は、黒が好きです。

PHRASE 13

私　は、かん国　へ　行きます。

Watashi wa, Kankoku e ikimasu.

I [PART] South Korea to to go = I will go to South Korea.

COPY THE JAPANESE SENTENCE:

VOCABULARY:

かん国 **Kankoku** = South Korea

へ **e** = to

イタリア **Itaria** = Italy

タイ **Tai** = Thailand

行きます **ikimasu** = to go

とうきょう **Tōkyō** = Tokyo

▪ **NOTES** ▪

The particle え **E** written as へ follows the pattern of PLACE へ行きます **E ikimasu.** You can also use the particle に **NI** interchangeably and write PLACE に行きます **NI ikimasu.**

WRITE THE FOLLOWING IN JAPANESE:

1. I will go to Tokyo.

2. I will go to Thailand.

3. I will go to Italy.

1. 私は、とうきょうへ行きます。
2. 私は、タイへ行きます。
3. 私は、イタリアに行きます。

PHRASE 14

私 は、 ご飯 を 食べます。

Watashi wa, gohan o tabemasu.

I [PART] cooked rice [PART] to eat = I eat rice.

COPY THE JAPANESE SENTENCE:

VOCABULARY:

ご飯 **gohan** = (cooked) rice

パン **pan** = bread

やさい **yasai** = vegetables

食べます **tabemasu** = to eat

▪ NOTES ▪

In Japanese, ごはん **gohan** refers to cooked rice, and こめ **kome** to uncooked rice.

WRITE THE FOLLOWING IN JAPANESE:

1. I will eat rice.

____

____

2. I will eat bread.

____

____

3. I will eat vegetables.

____

____

1. 私は、ご飯を食べます。
2. 私は、パンを食べます。
3. 私は、やさいを食べます。

PHRASE 15

私　は、お水　を　飲みます。

Watashi wa, o-mizu o nomimasu.

I [PART] water [PART] to drink = I drink water.

COPY THE JAPANESE SENTENCE:

VOCABULARY:

お水 **o-mizu** = water

お茶 **o-cha** = (Japanese) tea

コーヒー **kōhī** = coffee

飲みます **nomimasu** = to drink

▪ NOTES ▪

In Japanese, the word for Japanese green tea is お茶 **o-cha** and the word for black tea is こう茶 **kōcha**.

WRITE THE FOLLOWING IN JAPANESE:

1. I will drink water.

2. I will drink coffee.

3. I will drink Japanese tea.

1. 私は、お水を飲みます。
2. 私は、コーヒーを飲みます。
3. 私は、お茶を飲みます。

PHRASE 16

母　は、ひこうき　で　日本　へ　行きます。

Haha wa, hikōki de Nihon e ikimasu.

My mom [PART] airplane [PART] Japan to to go

= My mom will go to Japan by airplane.

COPY THE JAPANESE SENTENCE:

VOCABULARY:

ひこうき **hikōki** = airplane

車 **kuruma** = car

ちかてつ **chikatetsu** = subway

学校 **gakkō** = school

しんかんせん **shinkansen** = bullet train

▪ NOTES ▪

In major Japanese cities like Tokyo and Osaka, most people take public transportation which is very efficient and easy to figure out.

WRITE THE FOLLOWING IN JAPANESE:

1. I will go to Tokyo by bullet train.

____

____

2. I will go to school by subway.

____

____

3. I will go to school by car.

____

____

1. 私は、しんかんせんでとうきょうへ行きます。
2. 私は、ちかてつで学校へ行きます。
3. 私は、車で学校へ行きます。

PHRASE 17

父　は、ロシア　に　住んでいます。

Chichi wa, Roshia ni sundeimasu.

My dad [PART] Russia [PART] is living = My dad lives in Russia.

COPY THE JAPANESE SENTENCE:

VOCABULARY:

父 **chichi** = my dad

住んでいます **sundeimasu** = is living

ロシア **Roshia** = Russia

ナイジェリア **Naijeria** = Nigeria

メキシコ **Mekishiko** = Mexico

▪ NOTES ▪

You can add 語 **GO** to the Japanese word for a country to make a new word for the language, such as 日本語 **Nihon-go** for Japanese (language). You can also add 人 **jin** to the same word to make it a nationality, such as 日本人 **Nihonjin** for Japanese citizen.

WRITE THE FOLLOWING IN JAPANESE:

1. I am living in Nigeria.

2. I am living in Russia.

3. I am living in Mexico.

1. 私は、ナイジェリアに住んでいます。
2. 私は、ロシアに住んでいます。
3. 私は、メキシコに住んでいます。

PHRASE 18

私　は、電話　で　友だち　と　話します。

Watashi wa, denwa de tomodachi to hanashimasu.

I [PART] telephone [PART] friend [PART] to speak

= I speak on the phone with my friend.

COPY THE JAPANESE SENTENCE:

VOCABULARY:

友だち **tomodachi** = friend

電話 **denwa** = telephone

けいたい電話 **keitai-denwa** = cell phone

スマホ **sumaho** = smartphone

▪ NOTES ▪

Since most people use public transportation in major cities, they usually use different apps that show them the arrival times of trains and subways, and where to transfer. These even give information on which platform to catch the next train.

WRITE THE FOLLOWING IN JAPANESE:

1. I talk on the phone with my dad.

____

____

2. I talk on the cell phone with my friend.

____

____

3. I talk on the smartphone with my mom.

____

____

1. 私は、電話で父と話します。
2. 私は、けいたい電話で友だちと話します。
3. 私は、スマホで母と話します。

PHRASE 19

私 の しゅ味 は、テニス です。

Watashi no shumi wa, tenisu desu.

I [PART] hobby [PART] tennis [COPULA] = My hobby is tennis.

COPY THE JAPANESE SENTENCE:

VOCABULARY:

しゅ味 **shumi** = hobby

テニス **tenisu** = tennis

水泳 **suiei** = swimming

旅行 **ryokō** = traveling

▪ NOTES ▪

In order to form this sentence, the hobby must be in the noun form.

WRITE THE FOLLOWING IN JAPANESE:

1. My hobby is tennis.

2. My hobby is swimming.

3. My hobby is traveling.

1. 私のしゅ味は、テニスです。
2. 私のしゅ味は、水泳です。
3. 私のしゅ味は、旅行です。

PHRASE 20

犬 は、うち に います。

Inu wa, uchi ni imasu.

Dog [PART] house [PART] there is = The dog is at home.

COPY THE JAPANESE SENTENCE:

VOCABULARY:

うち **uchi** = house, home

犬 **inu** = dog

ねこ **neko** = cat

鳥 **tori** = bird

▪ NOTES ▪

In Japanese, there are two words for "there is." If the subject of the sentence is animate, such as an animal or a person, you use the word います **imasu**. However, if the subject is inanimate, such as a chair or a cup, you use the word あります **arimasu**.

WRITE THE FOLLOWING IN JAPANESE:

1. The dog is at school.

2. The cat is in Japan.

3. The bird is in the house.

1. 犬は、学校にいます。
2. ねこは、日本にいます。
3. 鳥は、うちにいます。

PHRASE 21

えんぴつ は、つくえ に あります。

Enpitsu **wa,** **tsukue** **ni** **arimasu.**

Pencil [PART] desk [PART] there is

= The pencil is on the desk.

COPY THE JAPANESE SENTENCE:

VOCABULARY:

えんぴつ **enpitsu** = pencil

つくえ **tsukue** = desk

お手洗い **o-tearai** = bathroom

あそこ **asoko** = over there

▪ NOTES ▪

It will be helpful to know these two kanji characters when you are looking for a bathroom in Japan: 男 **otoko** means "male" and 女 **onna** means "female." あそこ **asoko** refers to a place far from both speaker and listener. For more about あります **arimasu**, refer to Phrase 20 Notes.

WRITE THE FOLLOWING IN JAPANESE:

1. The bathroom is over there.

2. The telephone is on the desk.

3. The desk is over there.

1. お手洗いは、あそこにあります。
2. 電話は、つくえにあります。
3. つくえは、あそこにあります。

PHRASE 22

学校　に、先生　が　います。

Gakkō　ni,　sensei　ga　imasu.

School [PART] teacher [PART] there is = The teacher is at school.

COPY THE JAPANESE SENTENCE:

VOCABULARY:

女の子 **onna no ko** = girl

男の子 **otoko no ko** = boy

先生 **sensei** = teacher

魚 **sakana** = fish

▪ NOTES ▪

This sentence structure is very similar to the previous one. However, this sentence structure emphasizes the object, whereas the previous sentence structure emphasizes the place. For います **imasu**, see NOTES on phrase 20.

WRITE THE FOLLOWING IN JAPANESE:

1. The girl is in Russia.

2. The fish is at home.

3. The boy is over there.

1. ロシアに、女の子がいます。
2. うちに、魚がいます。
3. あそこに、男の子がいます。

PHRASE 23

ここ に、飲み物 が あります。

Koko ni, nomimono ga arimasu.

Here [PART] drinks [PART] there is = The drink is here.

COPY THE JAPANESE SENTENCE:

VOCABULARY:

飲み物 **nomimono** = drinks

ここ **koko** = here

食べ物 **tabemono** = food

木 **ki** = tree

▪ NOTES ▪

At a typical Japanese restaurant, you may see a replica of most, if not all, of the food items on the display window at the entrance. If you are still learning the language, you can use the display to point to what you would like to order.

WRITE THE FOLLOWING IN JAPANESE:

1. The tree is in the school.

2. The food is here.

3. The school is over there.

1. 学校に、木があります。
2. ここに、食べ物があります。
3. あそこに、学校があります。

PHRASE 24

私　は、日本　へ　行きたい　です。

Watashi wa, Nihon e ikitai desu.

I [PART] Japan to want to go [COPULA] = I want to go to Japan.

COPY THE JAPANESE SENTENCE:

VOCABULARY:

見ます **mimasu** = to watch, to look

テレビ **terebi** = TV

えいが **eiga** = movies

ブラジル **Burajiru** = Brazil

▪ NOTES ▪

行きたい **Ikitai** is formed using the verb stem (the verb in the ます **MASU** form minus **MASU**) and adding たい **tai**. To say "want to eat" you will take ます **masu** off of 食べます **tabemasu** and add たい **tai**, which becomes 食べたい **tabetai**.

WRITE THE FOLLOWING IN JAPANESE:

1. I want to go to Brazil.

2. I want to watch TV.

3. I want to watch a movie.

1. 私は、ブラジルへ行きたいです。
2. 私は、テレビが見たいです。
3. 私は、えいがが見たいです。

PHRASE 25

私　は、車　が　ほしい　です。

Watashi wa, kuruma ga hoshii desu.

I [PART] car [PART] want [COPULA] = I want a car.

COPY THE JAPANESE SENTENCE:

VOCABULARY:

ほしい **hoshii** = want, desire (n.)

お金 **okane** = money

花 **hana** = flower

おはし **ohashi** = chopsticks

▪ NOTES ▪

This form of "want" can only be used with nouns, whereas the たい **TAI** form can only be used with verbs.

WRITE THE FOLLOWING IN JAPANESE:

1. I want chopsticks.

2. I want flowers.

3. I want (some) money.

1. 私は、おはしがほしいです。
2. 私は、花がほしいです。
3. 私は、お金がほしいです。

PHRASE 26

私　は、ねこ　も　犬　も　好き　です。

Watashi wa, neko mo inu mo suki desu.

I [PART] cat and dog also like [COPULA]

= I like both cats and dogs.

COPY THE JAPANESE SENTENCE:

VOCABULARY:

牛にゅう **gyūnyū** = milk

ざっし **zasshi** = magazine

新聞 **shinbun** = newspaper

カナダ **Kanada** = Canada

▪ NOTES ▪

What is in front of each of the も **MO** must be in the noun form. Later on, you will learn how to change verbs into the noun form.

WRITE THE FOLLOWING IN JAPANESE:

1. I like both Canada and France.

2. I like both milk and tea.

3. I like both newspapers and magazines.

1. カナダもフランスも好きです。
2. 牛にゅうもお茶も好きです。
3. 新聞もざっしも好きです。

PHRASE 27

ざっし を 読み ませんか。

Zasshi o yomi masen ka.

Magazine [PART] to read will not [QUESTION FORM]

= Won't you read a magazine?

COPY THE JAPANESE SENTENCE:

VOCABULARY:

読みます **yomimasu** = to read

えいがかん **eiga-kan** = movie theater

ばんご飯 **ban-gohan** = dinner

どうが **dōga** = movie clip

▪ NOTES ▪

You form this sentence structure by taking off the す **SU** at the end of the verb and adding せんか **SEN KA**. This form is also called the invitational. [E.g. よみます **yomimaSU** + せんか **SEN KA** = よみませんか **yomimasen ka.**]

WRITE THE FOLLOWING IN JAPANESE:

1. Won't you eat dinner?

____

____

2. Won't you go to the movie theater?

____

____

3. Won't you watch a movie clip?

____

____

1. ばんご飯を食べませんか。
2. えいがかんへ行きませんか。
3. どうがを見ませんか。

PHRASE 28

日本　へ　行き　ましょう。

Nihon e iki mashō.

Japan to to go let's = Let's go to Japan.

COPY THE JAPANESE SENTENCE:

VOCABULARY:

〜ましょう **-mashō** = let's (do)

と書かん **toshokan** = library

銀行 **ginkō** = bank

おひるご飯 **ohiru-gohan** = lunch

▪ NOTES ▪

You form this sentence structure by taking off the す **SU** at the end of the verb and adding しょう **shō**. This form is also called the volitional form. [E.g. 行きます **ikimaSU** + しょう **shō** = 行きましょう **ikimashō**.]

WRITE THE FOLLOWING IN JAPANESE:

1. Let's go to the library.

2. Let's go to the bank.

3. Let's eat lunch.

1. と書かんへ行きましょう。
2. 銀行へ行きましょう。
3. おひるご飯を食べましょう。

PHRASE 29

プール　へ　行き　ましょうか。

Pūru e iki mashō ka.

Pool to to go shall we [QUESTION FORM] = Shall we go to the pool?

COPY THE JAPANESE SENTENCE:

VOCABULARY:

〜ましょうか **-mashō ka** = shall we ~

プール **pūru** = pool

レストラン **resutoran** = restaurant

朝ご飯 **asa-gohan** = breakfast

ジュース **jūsu** = juice

▪ NOTES ▪

This form 〜ましょうか **-mashō ka** is used to politely suggest to another person what you want to do together.

WRITE THE FOLLOWING IN JAPANESE:

1. Shall we drink (some) juice?

2. Shall we eat breakfast?

3. Shall we eat at a restaurant?

1. ジュースを飲みましょうか。
2. 朝ご飯を食べましょうか。
3. レストランで食べましょうか。

PHRASE 30

私 は、生徒 でした。

Watashi wa, seito deshita.

I [PART] student [COPULA IN PAST TENSE] = I was a student.

COPY THE JAPANESE SENTENCE:

VOCABULARY:

生徒 **seito** = non-college student

子ども **kodomo** = child

静か **shizuka** = is quiet

先生 **sensei** = teacher

▪ NOTES ▪

でした **DESHITA** is the past tense of です **DESU**. Remember, the tenses are at the very end in Japanese sentences. You can change the meaning of a sentence with the verb ending used.

WRITE THE FOLLOWING IN JAPANESE:

1. My dad was a teacher.

2. I was a child.

3. I was quiet.

1. 父は、先生でした。
2. 私は、子どもでした。
3. 私は、しずかでした。

PHRASE 31

私　は、朝ご飯　に　たまご　を　食べました。

Watashi wa, asa-gohan ni tamago o tabemashita.

I [PART] breakfast [PART] eggs [PART] ate

= I ate eggs for breakfast.

COPY THE JAPANESE SENTENCE:

VOCABULARY:

ベーコン **bēkon** = bacon

りんご **ringo** = apple

たまご **tamago** = egg

ソーセージ **sōsēji** = sausage

▪ NOTES ▪

After a meal, you will use the particle に **NI** to mean "for." You can use this after breakfast, lunch, and dinner. Remember, 食べました **tabemashita** is the past tense form of 食べます **tabemasu**.

WRITE THE FOLLOWING IN JAPANESE:

1. I ate bacon for breakfast.

2. I will eat sausages for breakfast.

3. I ate an apple for breakfast.

1. 私は、朝ご飯にベーコンを食べました。
2. 私は、朝ご飯にソーセージを食べます。
3. 私は、朝ご飯にりんごを食べました。

PHRASE 32

私　は、おひるご飯　に　ハンバーガー　を　食べます。

Watashi wa, ohiru-gohan ni hanbāgā o tabemasu.

I [PART] lunch [PART] hamburger [PART] to eat

= I will eat a hamburger for lunch.

COPY THE JAPANESE SENTENCE:

VOCABULARY:

おひるご飯 **ohiru-gohan** = lunch

ポテトフライ **potetofurai** = French fries

サラダ **sarada** = salad

なべ物 **nabemono** = hot pot

ハンバーガー **hanbaga** = hamburger

▪ NOTES ▪

There are a lot of different types of Japanese hot pots including なべ物 **nabemono**, しゃぶしゃぶ **shabu shabu**, すきやき **sukiyaki**, and おでん **oden**. They are favorites for many, especially when it is cold. You can set up a grill on the dinner table so that you can enjoy freshly made food that's cooked right at the table.

WRITE THE FOLLOWING IN JAPANESE:

1. I ate hot pot for lunch.

2. I will eat French fries for lunch.

3. I ate salad for lunch.

1. 私は、おひるご飯になべ物を食べました。
2. 私は、おひるご飯にポテトフライを食べます。
3. 私は、おひるご飯にサラダを食べました。

PHRASE 33

私　は、ばんご飯　に　　　もち　　を　食べます。

Watashi wa, ban-gohan ni mochi o tabemasu.

I [PART] dinner [PART] pounded rice cakes [PART] to eat

= I will eat pounded rice cakes for dinner.

COPY THE JAPANESE SENTENCE:

VOCABULARY:

ばんご飯 **ban-gohan** = dinner

もち **mochi** = pounded rice cakes

アイスクリーム **aisukurīmu** = ice cream

ギョーザ **gyōza** = potstickers

▪ NOTES ▪

ギョーザ **Gyōza** is a very popular food in Japan, often served in ramen restaurants. Each place has their own recipe and ギョーザ **gyōza** can either be boiled or pan fried. It is often dipped in soy sauce, vinegar and hot oil called ラーゆ **rāyu**.

WRITE THE FOLLOWING IN JAPANESE:

1. I will eat potstickers for dinner.

2. I will drink water for dinner.

3. I will eat ice cream for dinner.

1.私は、ばんご飯にギョーザを食べます。
2.私は、ばんご飯に水を飲みます。
3.私は、ばんご飯にアイスクリームを食べます。

PHRASE 34

おなか が いたい です。

Onaka ga itai desu.

Stomach [PART] painful [COPULA] = I have a stomachache.

COPY THE JAPANESE SENTENCE:

VOCABULARY:

おなか **onaka** = stomach

いたい **itai** = is painful, is sore

頭 **atama** = head

は **ha** = tooth, teeth

手 **te** = hand

▪ NOTES ▪

As you notice with the word, は **HA** it means both "tooth" and "teeth." In Japanese, there is no plural form for words.

WRITE THE FOLLOWING IN JAPANESE:

1. I have a toothache.

2. I have a headache.

3. My hand hurts.

1. はがいたいです。
2. 頭がいたいです。
3. 手がいたいです。

PHRASE 35

私　の　友だち　は、テニス　が　じょうず　です。

Watashi	**no**	**tomodachi**	**wa,**	**tenisu**	**ga**	**jōzu**	**desu.**
I	[PART]	friend	[PART]	tennis	[PART]	skillful	[COPULA]

= My friend is skillful at tennis.

COPY THE JAPANESE SENTENCE:

VOCABULARY:

じょうず **jōzu** = is skillful, is good at

友だち **tomodachi** = friend

サッカー **sakkā** = soccer

ダンス **dansu** = dance

やきゅう **yakyū** = baseball

▪ NOTES ▪

Particle の **NO** can be translated as "'s" to show possession. To show humbleness you do not use じょうず **JŌZU** meaning "skillful" to describe yourself.

WRITE THE FOLLOWING IN JAPANESE:

1. My friend is skillful at baseball.

____

____

2. My friend is skillful at soccer.

____

____

3. My friend is skillful at dance.

____

____

1. 私のともだちは、やきゅうがじょうずです。
2. 私のともだちは、サッカーがじょうずです。
3. 私のともだちは、ダンスがじょうずです。

PHRASE 36

昨日、私 は えいが を 見ました。

Kinō, watashi wa eiga o mimashita.

Yesterday, I [PART] movies [PART] watched

= I watched a movie yesterday.

COPY THE JAPANESE SENTENCE:

VOCABULARY:

昨日 **kinō** = yesterday

あそびます **asobimasu** = to play

聞きます **kikimasu** = to listen

ラジオ **rajio** = radio

▪ NOTES ▪

In Japanese, tenses are at the very end of the sentence. For past tense, you change from the ます **MASU** form to the ました **MASHITA** form.

WRITE THE FOLLOWING IN JAPANESE:

1. I played in school yesterday.

2. I drank milk yesterday.

3. I listened to the radio yesterday.

1. 昨日、私は、学校であそびました。
2. 昨日、私は、牛にゅうを飲みました。
3. 昨日、私は、ラジオを聞きました。

PHRASE 37

私　は、おどりません。

Watashi wa, odorimasen.

I [PART] not dance = I do not dance.

COPY THE JAPANESE SENTENCE:

VOCABULARY:

おどります **odorimasu** = to dance

買います **kaimasu** = to buy

書きます **kakimasu** = to write

母 **haha** = my mother

父 **chichi** = my father, my dad

手紙 **tegami** = letter

▪ NOTES ▪

In Japanese, there are humble terms for family members that you use when talking about your own family members to others. However, when talking directly to your family members, you would use the respectful terms.

WRITE THE FOLLOWING IN JAPANESE:

1. I will not buy a flower.

2. My mother will not drink coffee.

3. My father will not write a letter.

1. 私は、花を買いません。
2. 母は、コーヒーを飲みません。
3. 父は、手紙を書きません。

PHRASE 38

母　は、中国　に　行きません　でした。

Haha wa, Chūgoku ni ikimasen deshita.

My mother [PART] China [PART] not go [COPULA IN PAST TENSE]

= My mother did not go to China.

COPY THE JAPANESE SENTENCE:

VOCABULARY:

帰ります **kaerimasu** = to return

来ます **kimasu** = to come

兄 **ani** = my older brother

姉 **ane** = my older sister

かちます **kachimasu** = to win

▪ NOTES ▪

In Japanese, there are three directional verbs that are very distinct. 行きます **IKIMASU** is to go, 来ます **KIMASU** is "to come," and 帰ります **KAERIMASU** is "to return." 帰ります **KAERIMASU** denotes that you have returned to the place you came from, like your own home.

WRITE THE FOLLOWING IN JAPANESE:

1. My older brother did not return home yesterday.

2. My friend did not come to my house.

3. My older sister did not win.

1. 兄は、昨日うちに帰りませんでした。
2. 私の友だちは、うちに来ませんでした。
3. 姉は、かちませんでした。

PHRASE 39

私　の　友だち　は、うち　に　来て、あそびました。

Watashi no tomodachi wa, uchi ni kite, asobimashita.

I [PART] friend [PART] house [PART] to come played

= My friend came to my house to play.

COPY THE JAPANESE SENTENCE:

VOCABULARY:

します **shimasu** = to do

会社 **kaisha** = company

料理をします **ryōri o shimasu** = to cook

おどります **odorimasu** = to dance

はたらきます **hatarakimasu** = to work

▪ NOTES ▪

The **TE** form of a verb, also known as the gerund form, can be used in many ways, like joining multiple verbs in one sentence. Japanese verbs are grouped into Group 1, Group 2 and Group 3 verbs. See page viii for more on Japanese verbs.

WRITE THE FOLLOWING IN JAPANESE:

1. I cooked and watched TV.

2. My mom came to school and danced.

3. My older brother will go to his company and work.

1. 私は、料理をして、テレビを見ました。
2. 母は、学校へ来て、おどりました。
3. 兄は、会社に行って、はたらきます。

PHRASE 40

父　は、テレビ　を　見て、わらいました。

Chichi wa, terebi o mite, waraimashita.

My father [PART] TV [PART] to watch laughed

= My father watched TV and laughed.

COPY THE JAPANESE SENTENCE:

VOCABULARY:

わらいます **waraimasu** = to laugh

なきます **nakimasu** = to cry

おきます **okimasu** = to wake up

道にまよいます **michi ni mayoimasu** = to lose my way

おそくなります **osokunarimasu** = to be late

▪ NOTES ▪

The verbs on this page are Group 2 verbs, and have え **E** before ます **MASU**, except for 起きます **okimasu** where it is い **I** before ます **MASU**. Refer to page ix on how to change Group 2 verbs into the て **TE** form.

WRITE THE FOLLOWING IN JAPANESE:

1. My older brother woke up and ate breakfast.

____

____

2. My older sister watched a movie and cried.

____

____

3. I lost my way and returned home late.

____

____

1. 兄は、おきて、あさご飯を食べました。
2. 姉は、えいがを見て、なきました。
3. 私は、道にまよって、うちへ帰るのがおそくなりました。

PHRASE 41

兄　　は、お水　を　飲んで、ねました。

Ani　　wa,　omizu　o　nonde,　nemashita.

My older brother [PART] water [PART] to drink slept

= My older brother drank water and then slept.

COPY THE JAPANESE SENTENCE:

VOCABULARY:

ねます **nemasu** = to sleep

走ります **hashirimasu** = to run

歩きます **arukimasu** = to walk

買います **kaimasu** = to buy

泳ぎます **oyogimasu** = to swim

▪ NOTES ▪

The verbs on this page are Group 1 verbs, and have い **I** before ます **MASU**. Refer to page ix on how to change Group 1 verbs into the て **TE** form.

WRITE THE FOLLOWING IN JAPANESE:

1. My older brother went to Japan to run.

____

____

2. My older sister swam and won.

____

____

3. I walked and bought milk.

____

____

1. 兄は、日本に行って、走りました。
2. 姉は、泳いで、かちました。
3. 私は、あるいて、ぎゅうにゅうを買いました。

PHRASE 42

私　は　すわって、本　を　読みました。

Watashi wa suwatte, hon o yomimashita.

I [PART] to sit, book [PART] read [PAST TENSE]

= I sat and read a book.

COPY THE JAPANESE SENTENCE:

VOCABULARY:

すわります **suwarimasu** = to sit

本 **hon** = book

べんとう **bentō** = box lunch

おにぎり **onigiri** = rice ball

明日 **ashita** = tomorrow

▪ **NOTES** ▪

This page will incorporate the three groups of Japanese verbs. Refer to page ix which shows how て **TE** forms are created for each group.

WRITE THE FOLLOWING IN JAPANESE:

1. My friend ate a rice ball and drank tea.

2. My dog ran and drank water.

3. I will go to the library and read a book.

1. 私の友だちは、おにぎりを食べて、お茶を飲みました。
2. 私の犬は、走って、水を飲みました。
3. 私は、と書かんへ行って、本を読みます。

PHRASE 43

学校　へ　行って　ください。

Gakkō　e　itte　kudasai.

School　to　to go　please　= Please go to school.

COPY THE JAPANESE SENTENCE:

VOCABULARY:

ドア **doa** = door

窓 **mado** = window

閉めます **shimemasu** = to close

開けます **akemasu** = to open

洗たくをします **sentaku o shimasu** = to do laundry

ください **Kudasai** means "please" in Japanese. て **TE** + ください **KUDASAI** sentences imply making requests of someone to do something. ください **Kudasai** is at the end of a sentence, as it is considered a verb.

WRITE THE FOLLOWING IN JAPANESE:

1. Please open the window.

2. Please close the door.

3. Please do the laundry.

1. 窓を開けてください。
2. ドアを閉めてください。
3. 洗たくをしてください。

PHRASE 44

この ケーキ を 食べて も いい ですか。

Kono kēki o tabete mo ii desu ka.

This cake [PART] to eat [PART] can [COPULA QUESTION]

= May I eat this cake?

COPY THE JAPANESE SENTENCE:

VOCABULARY:

パリ **Pari** = Paris

早く **hayaku** = early

この **kono** = this (noun)

ケーキ **kēki** = cake

▪ NOTES ▪

いい **ii** means "good." て **TE** + いい **II** in a sentence is a polite phrase asking the listener's permission to do something.

WRITE THE FOLLOWING IN JAPANESE:

1. May I go to Paris?

____

____

2. May I sleep early?

____

____

3. May I buy this book?

____

____

1. パリへ行ってもいいですか。
2. 早くねてもいいですか。
3. この本を買ってもいいですか。

PHRASE 45

窓　を　開けて　は、いけません。

Mado　o　akete　wa,　ikemasen.

Window [PART] to open [PART] may not

= You may not open the window.

COPY THE JAPANESE SENTENCE:

VOCABULARY:

いけません **ikemasen** = may not

うたいます **utaimasu** = to sing

大学 **daigaku** = college

うんてんをします **unten o shimasu** = to drive

かけます **kakemasu** = to call

▪ NOTES ▪

Each culture has different things that are frowned upon that may be totally acceptable in another country. For example, in Japan it is not acceptable to walk around in a house with your shoes, or to put your hands in your pockets especially in official situations.

WRITE THE FOLLOWING IN JAPANESE:

1. You may not sing at school.

2. You may not drive in the college.

3. You may not eat in the library.

1. 学校でうたっては、いけません。
2. 大学でうんてんをしては、いけません。
3. と書かんで食べては、いけません。

PHRASE 46

犬　は、今　走っています。

Inu　wa,　ima　hashitteimasu.

Dog [PART] now running = The dog is running right now.

COPY THE JAPANESE SENTENCE:

VOCABULARY:

今 **ima** = now

食どう **shokudō** = dining hall

のります **norimasu** = to ride

タクシー **takushī** = taxi

▪ NOTES ▪

ています **TEIMASU** is translated as *~ing* or the progressive aspect. The use of this verb form shows what is happening or the current state of action.

WRITE THE FOLLOWING IN JAPANESE:

1. My mother is riding a taxi.

____

____

2. My older sister is eating in the dining hall now.

____

____

3. I am running at school.

____

____

1. 母は、今タクシーにのっています。
2. 姉は、今食どうで食べています。
3. 私は、今学校で走っています。

PHRASE 47

晩ご飯　を　食べて　から、宿題　をします。

Ban-gohan　o　tabete　kara, shukudai　o　shimasu.

Dinner [PART] to eat after, homework [PART] to do

= I will do homework after eating dinner.

COPY THE JAPANESE SENTENCE:

VOCABULARY:

宿題 **shukudai** = homework

おふろ **ofuro** = bath

入ります **hairimasu** = to go in

作文 **sakubun** = essay

▪ NOTES ▪

In Japan, people normally take a bath in the evening. The water in the bath tub is for everyone (the whole family) to use, so DO NOT flush away the water after you have finished your bath. BEFORE you go into the bath tub, do your cleaning and shampooing outside the tub.

WRITE THE FOLLOWING IN JAPANESE:

1. After taking (going in) a bath, I will sleep.

2. I will write the essay after reading the book.

3. I will go to school after eating breakfast.

1. おふろに入ってから、ねます。
2. 本を読んでから、作文を書きます。
3. あさご飯を食べてから、学校へ行きます。

PHRASE 48

私 は、まだ 本 を 読んでいません。

Watashi wa, mada hon o yondeimasen.

I [PART] yet book [PART] have not read

= I have not read the book yet.

COPY THE JAPANESE SENTENCE:

VOCABULARY:

まだ **mada** = yet

クイズ **kuizu** = quiz

勉強をします **benkyō o shimasu** = to study

シャワー **shawā** = shower

あびます **abimasu** = to shower

作ります **tsukurimasu** = to make

▪ NOTES ▪

Note the different verbs to use: "to take a bath" is おふろに入ります **ofuro ni hairimasu**, and "to take a shower" is シャワーをあびます **shawā o abimasu**.

WRITE THE FOLLOWING IN JAPANESE:

1. I have not studied for the quiz yet.

2. I have not taken a shower.

3. I have not made dinner yet.

1. 私は、まだクイズの勉強をしていません。
2. 私は、まだシャワーをあびていません。
3. 私は、まだ晩ご飯を作っていません。

PHRASE 49

おすし は、おいしい から 好き です。

O-sushi wa, oishii kara suki desu.

Sushi [PART] delicious so like [COPULA]

= I like sushi because it is delicious.

COPY THE JAPANESE SENTENCE:

VOCABULARY:

おすし **o-sushi** = sushi

おいしい **oishii** = is delicious

まずい **mazui** = is not tasty

やさい **yasai** = vegetable

きらい **kirai** = to dislike

楽しい **tanoshii** = is fun

おもしろい **omoshiroi** = is interesting

▪ NOTES ▪

から **kara** is translated as "because" or "so." When forming the sentences, it is easier to think of it as "**so**" because the reason comes first and then the result. Each half of a Japaense sentence is a sentence by itself.

WRITE THE FOLLOWING IN JAPANESE:

1. I don't like vegetables because they are not tasty.

____

____

2. I like school because it is fun.

____

____

3. I like my friend because she is interesting.

____

____

1. やさいはまずいから、きらいです。
2. 学校は楽しいから、好きです。
3. ともだちはおもしろいから、好きです。

PHRASE 50

私　は、レストラン　へ　食べ　に　行きます。

Watashi	**wa,**	**resutoran**	**e**	**tabe**	**ni**	**ikimasu.**
I	[PART]	restaurant	to	to eat	[PART]	to go

= I will go to the restaurant to eat.

COPY THE JAPANESE SENTENCE:

VOCABULARY:

デパート **depāto** = department store

勉強をします **benkyō o shimasu** = to study

買い物をします **kaimono o shimasu** = to shop

海 **umi** = beach/ocean

▪ NOTES ▪

The Japanese department stores are quite massive and you are able to find almost anything that you would like to buy. The bottom two basement floors are filled with food, drinks, and consumable gifts. There are many floors devoted to clothing, and the top floors are usually used for restaurants.

WRITE THE FOLLOWING IN JAPANESE:

1. My older sister will go to the department store to shop.

____

____

2. My father will go to the beach to swim.

____

____

3. I will go to school to study.

____

____

1. 姉は、デパートへ買い物に行きます。
2. 父は、海へ泳ぎに行きます。
3. 私は、学校へ勉強しに行きます。

PHRASE 51

私　は、　オランダ　しゅっしん　です。

Watashi wa, Oranda shusshin desu.

I [PART] the Netherlands person's origin [COPULA]

= I am from the Netherlands.

COPY THE JAPANESE SENTENCE:

VOCABULARY:

しゅっしん **shusshin** = a person's origin

オランダ **Oranda** = the Netherlands

オレゴン **Oregon** = Oregon

はかた **Hakata** = Hakata (city in Japan)

▪ **NOTES** ▪

Hakata is located in Fukuoka City, on the island of 九州 **Kyūshū**. It is one of the oldest cities in Japan and is known for its ラーメン **rāmen** and its beautiful port. It was a merchant town. It is now popular with cruise ships going to many countries including China and South Korea.

WRITE THE FOLLOWING IN JAPANESE:

1. I am from Oregon.

2. I am from Hakata.

3. I am from China.

1. 私は、オレゴンしゅっしんです。
2. 私は、はかたしゅっしんです。
3. 私は、中国しゅっしんです。

PHRASE 52

私 は、新聞 や ざっし など を 読みます。

Watashi wa, shinbun ya zasshi nado o yomimasu.

I [PART] newspaper and magazine such [PART] to read

= I read such things as newspapers and magazines.

COPY THE JAPANESE SENTENCE:

VOCABULARY:

インド **Indo** = India

スペイン語 **Supein-go** = Spanish language

ぶたまん **butaman** = pork buns

ギョーザ **gyōza** = potstickers

You can use the や **YA**, など **NADO** form to give a few examples from a list. It is similar to "etcetera" in English. Most of the time, you would use one or two や **YA** to give a few examples.

WRITE THE FOLLOWING IN JAPANESE:

1. I will go to the library, movie theater, etc.

2. My mom will go to India, China, etc.

3. My older sister speaks Spanish, English, etc.

1. 私は、としょかんやえいがかんなどへ行きます。
2. 母は、インドや中国などへ行きます。
3. 姉は、スペイン語や英語などを話します。

PHRASE 53

この 映画 は、おもしろく ない です。

Kono eiga wa, omoshiroku nai desu.

This movie [PART] interesting [NEGATIVE] [COPULA]

= This movie is not interesting.

COPY THE JAPANESE SENTENCE:

VOCABULARY:

良い/いい **yoi/ii** = is good

悪い **warui** = is bad

弟 **otōto** = my younger brother

妹 **imōto** = my younger sister

てんすう **tensū** = score

かわいい **kawaii** = is pretty, is cute

▪ NOTES ▪

Japanese adjectives are categorized as い **I** adjectives and な **NA** adjectives. The adjectives on this page are い **I** adjectives. To form negative い **I** adjectives, replace the い **i** with くない **kunai**. **Change いい **ii** to よい **yoi** before converting it to its negative form.

WRITE THE FOLLOWING IN JAPANESE:

1. My younger brother's scores are not bad.

2. My younger sister's cat is not cute.

3. This book is not interesting.

1. 弟のてんすうは、悪くないです。
2. 妹のねこは、かわいくないです。
3. この本は、おもしろくないです。

PHRASE 54

バスケットボール の しあい は、楽しかった です。

Basukettobōru no shiai wa, tanoshikatta desu.

Basketball [PART] game [PART] fun [past form] [COPULA]

= The basketball game was fun.

COPY THE JAPANESE SENTENCE:

____

____

____

VOCABULARY:

しあい **shiai** = game, match

かなしい **kanashii** = is sad

むずかしい **muzukashii** = is difficult

うれしい **ureshii** = is happy

今日 **kyō** = today

▪ NOTES ▪

To change い **I** adjectives to the past form, you will need to take off the い **i** and add かった **katta**.

WRITE THE FOLLOWING IN JAPANESE:

1. My younger brother was sad yesterday.

____

____

2. My younger sister was happy.

____

____

3. The homework was difficult today.

____

____

1. 弟は、昨日かなしかったです。
2. 妹は、うれしかったです。
3. 今日の宿題は、むずかしかったです。

PHRASE 55

日本 は、さむくなかった です。

Nihon wa, samuku nakatta desu.

Japan [PART] cold [NEGATIVE PAST] [COPULA] = Japan was not cold.

COPY THE JAPANESE SENTENCE:

VOCABULARY:

とおい **tōi** = is far

さむい **samui** = is cold

強い **tsuyoi** = is strong

あたたかい **atatakai** = is warm

▪ NOTES ▪

To change い **I** adjectives to the negative past form, you will need to take off the い **i** and add くなかった **kunakatta**.

WRITE THE FOLLOWING IN JAPANESE:

1. France was not far.

____

____

2. My friend was not strong.

____

____

3. Russia was not warm.

____

____

1. フランスは、とおくなかったです。
2. 私のともだちは、強くなかったです。
3. ロシアは、あたたかくなかったです。

PHRASE 56

私　は、今日　元気　じゃない　です。

Watashi　wa,　kyō　genki　ja nai　desu.

I　[PART]　today　fine　is not　[COPULA]　=　I am not fine today.

COPY THE JAPANESE SENTENCE:

VOCABULARY:

元気 **genki** = is healthy, fine

静か **shizuka** = is quiet

有名 **yūmei** = is famous

きれい **kirei** = is pretty, is clean

▪ NOTES ▪

The adjectives on this page are な **NA** adjectives. To change な **NA** adjectives to the past form, you will need to add じゃない **janai**. Please note that even though the following words end with an い **i** they are considered な adjectives: きれい **kirei**, きらい **kirai**, とくい **tokui**, ゆうめい **yūmei**.

WRITE THE FOLLOWING IN JAPANESE:

1. This beach is not clean.

2. My friend is not famous.

3. The dog is not quiet.

1. この海は、きれいじゃないです。
2. 私の友だちは、有名じゃないです。
3. 犬は、静かじゃないです。

PHRASE 57

この　しけん　は、大事　　でした。

Kono　shiken　wa,　daiji　　deshita.

This　exam　[PART]　important　[COPULA IN PAST TENSE]

= This exam was important.

COPY THE JAPANESE SENTENCE:

___

___

___

VOCABULARY:

大事 **daiji** = is important

じゃま **jama** = is in the way

だめ **dame** = is bad

しけん **shiken** = exam

▪ NOTES ▪

To change な **NA** adjectives to the past form, you will need to add でした **deshita**.

WRITE THE FOLLOWING IN JAPANESE:

1. My younger brother was in the way.

2. This exam was bad.

3. The library was quiet.

1. 弟は、じゃまでした。
2. このしけんは、だめでした。
3. と書かんは、静かでした。

PHRASE 58

この　けいけん　は、　いや　じゃなかった　です。

Kono	**keiken**	**wa,**	**iya**	**ja nakatta**	**desu.**
This	experience	[PART]	unpleasant	was not	[COPULA]

= This experience was not unpleasant.

COPY THE JAPANESE SENTENCE:

VOCABULARY:

いや **iya** = is unpleasant

けいけん **keiken** = experience

大ぜい **ōzei** = great number of people

駅 **eki** = train station

▪ NOTES ▪

To change な **NA** adjectives to their negative past form, you will need to add じゃなかった **janakatta**. Please note that 大ぜい **ōzei** is a な **NA** adjective even though it ends with an い **i**.

WRITE THE FOLLOWING IN JAPANESE:

1. The movie was not famous.

2. This exam was not bad.

3. The train station did not have a great number of people.

1. この映画は、有名じゃなかったです。
2. このしけんは、だめじゃなかったです。
3. 駅は、人が大ぜいじゃなかったです。

PHRASE 59

食べすぎて、おなか が いたい です。

Tabe sugite, onaka ga itai desu.

Eat too much, stomach [PART] painful [COPULA]

= My stomach hurts because I ate too much.

COPY THE JAPANESE SENTENCE:

VOCABULARY:

すぎます **sugimasu** = too much

ビール **bīru** = beer

おかし **okashi** = sweets

高い **takai** = is tall; is expensive

▪ NOTES ▪

すぎます **Sugimasu**, meaning "to go beyond, to be excessive" has its **TE** form attached to a verb stem (たべ **tabe** in this example) to mean something is done in an excessive manner. 食べすぎて **Tabesugite** means "to overeat." Please note that すぎます **sugimasu** is a special Group 2 verb so the て **TE** form is すぎて **sugite**.

WRITE THE FOLLOWING IN JAPANESE:

1. The car is too expensive.

2. I ate too much of the sweets.

3. Yesterday, I drank too much beer.

3. 昨日、ビールを飲みすぎました。
2. おかしを食べすぎました。
1. その車は高すぎます。

PHRASE 60

私　は、月曜日　に　日本　に　行きます。

Watashi wa, Getsu-yōbi ni Nihon ni ikimasu.

I [PART] Monday [PART] Japan [PART] to go

= I will go to Japan on Monday.

COPY THE JAPANESE SENTENCE:

VOCABULARY:

月曜日 **Getsu-yōbi** = Monday

火曜日 **Ka-yōbi** = Tuesday

水曜日 **Sui-yōbi** = Wednesday

木曜日 **Moku-yōbi** = Thursday

金曜日 **Kin-yōbi** = Friday

土曜日 **Do-yōbi** = Saturday

日曜日 **Nichi-yōbi** = Sunday

▪ NOTES ▪

Each of the kanji characters used for the days of the week also corresponds to a basic natural element such as the moon, fire, and water.

WRITE THE FOLLOWING IN JAPANESE:

1. On Tuesday, I ate Chinese noodles in soup.

2. On Saturday, I will buy a car.

3. On Friday, my older brother returned home.

1. 私は、火曜日にラーメンを食べました。
2. 私は、土曜日に車を買います。
3. 兄は、金曜日にうちに帰りました。

PHRASE 61

私 は、五時 に 晩ご飯 を 食べました。

Watashi wa, go-ji ni ban-gohan o tabemashita.

I [PART] 5:00 [PART] dinner [PART] ate

= I ate dinner at 5:00.

COPY THE JAPANESE SENTENCE:

VOCABULARY:

一時 **ichi-ji** =1:00

五時 **go-ji** = 5:00

半 **han** = half past

十時 **jū-ji** =10:00

四時 **yo-ji** = 4:00

九時半 **ku-ji han** = 9:30

▪ NOTES ▪

In order to say the time, you will need to say the number plus 時 **ji** for the hour. We need to pay attention to the number 4 when used with time. For time, we say 四時 **yo-ji** (4:00), not **shi-ji**, because **shi** is considered unlucky, as it has the same sound as the word for death.

WRITE THE FOLLOWING IN JAPANESE:

1. At 10:00, I will go to the department store.

2. At 9:30, I will drink milk.

3. At 4:00, I will meet a friend.

1. 私は、十時にデパートに行きます。
2. 私は、九時半に牛にゅうを飲みます。
3. 私は、四時に友だちに会います。

PHRASE 62

私　は、午後　四時　五分　に　うち　へ　帰りました。

Watashi wa, gogo yo-ji go-fun ni uchi e kaerimashita.

I [PART] PM 4:00 5 minutes [PART] house to returned

= I returned home at 4:05 PM.

COPY THE JAPANESE SENTENCE:

____

____

____

VOCABULARY:

いっぷん/一分 **ip-pun** = 1 minute

さんぷん/三分 **san-pun** = 3 minutes

ごふん/五分 **go-fun** = 5 minutes

午後 **gogo** = PM

午前 **gozen** = AM

▪ NOTES ▪

The Japanese word for "minutes" is **fun** or **pun**. For 2, 5, 7 or 9 minutes use 分 **fun**; for 1, 6, 8, and 10, use the double sound denoted by with the basic number, e.g. 6 minutes is 六分 **rop-pun**. All other timing in minutes will end with ぷん **pun**.

WRITE THE FOLLOWING IN JAPANESE:

1. At 7:01 AM, I will wake up.

____

____

2. At 8:15 PM, I ate dinner.

____

____

3. At 3:03 PM, my friend came.

____

____

1. 私は、午前七時一分におきます。
2. 私は、午後八時十五分に晩ご飯を食べました。
3. 友だちは、午後三時三分に来ました。

PHRASE 63

私　は、一時　から二時　まで　れきし　を　勉強します。

Watashi wa, ichi-ji kara ni-ji made rekishi o benkyō shimasu.

I [PART] 1:00 from 2:00 until history [PART] study to do

= I will study history from 1:00 to 2:00.

COPY THE JAPANESE SENTENCE:

VOCABULARY:

れきし **rekishi** = history

かがく **kagaku** = science

すうがく **sūgaku** = math

びじゅつ **bijutsu** = art

▪ NOTES ▪

In Japanese schools, students often help clean the hallways and their homerooms. There are also cubbyholes in the entrance for students to leave their shoes, after which they change into their slippers. This helps them not track mud and dirt into the building.

WRITE THE FOLLOWING IN JAPANESE:

1. I will study art from 9:00 to 10:00.

2. I will study math from 11:00 to 12:00.

3. My younger brother will study science from 8:00 to 9:30.

1. 私は、九時から十時までびじゅつを勉強します。
2. 私は、十一時から十二時まですうがくを勉強します。
3. 弟は、八時から九時半までかがくを勉強します。

PHRASE 64

私　は、パーティー　を　楽しみ　に　しています。

Watashi wa, pātī o tanoshimi ni shiteimasu.

I [PART] party [PART] fun [PART] doing

= I am looking forward to the party.

COPY THE JAPANESE SENTENCE:

VOCABULARY:

楽しみにしています **tanoshimi ni shiteimasu** = looking forward to

お正月 **o-shōgatsu** = New Year's

クリスマス **kurisumasu** = Christmas

たん生日 **tanjōbi** = birthday

▪ NOTES ▪

In Japan, the New Year holiday is the biggest holiday of the year. On New Year's Eve, families usually go to the temples and shrines. Soba noodles are usually eaten then. During the New Year holidays a special meal called おせちりょうり **Osechiyōri** is eaten.

WRITE THE FOLLOWING IN JAPANESE:

1. I am looking forward to New Year's.

2. I am looking forward to Christmas.

3. I am looking forward to my birthday.

1. 私は、お正月を楽しみにしています。
2. 私は、クリスマスを楽しみにしています。
3. 私は、たん生日を楽しみにしています。

PHRASE 65

昨日　は、何　を　食べました　か。

Kinō wa, nani o tabemashita ka.

Yesterday [PART] what [PART] ate [QUESTION FORM]

= What did you eat yesterday?

COPY THE JAPANESE SENTENCE:

VOCABULARY:

何 **nani/nan** = what

何人 **nanijin** = what nationality

かれ **kare** = he, him

何時 **nan-ji** = what time

何人 **nan'nin** = how many people

何曜日 **nan-yōbi** = what day of the week

Forming questions in Japanese is quite easy. You keep the basic sentence structure and replace what you are trying to find out with a question word and add か **KA** at the end of the sentence. There are two ways to say "what" in Japanese: なに **nani** and なん **nan**. It depends on the sentence. The receiver of the question is implied: it usually means the listener or "you."

WRITE THE FOLLOWING IN JAPANESE:

1. What's his nationality?

2. What time is it now?

3. How many students are there?

1. かれは、何人(なにじん)ですか。
2. 今、何時ですか。
3. 生徒は、何人(なんにん)ですか。

PHRASE 66

駅　　は、どこ　ですか。

Eki　wa,　doko　desu ka.

Train station [PART] where [COPULA QUESTION] = Where is the train station?

COPY THE JAPANESE SENTENCE:

VOCABULARY:

どこ **doko** = where

かいだん **kaidan** = stairs

ゆうびん局 **yūbinkyoku** = post office

さいふ **saifu** = wallet

▪ NOTES ▪

Answering questions is also easy. You listen to the question word (e.g. なん **nan** or なに **nani**) and insert the answer in place of the question word, and also take off the か **ka** at the end.

WRITE THE FOLLOWING IN JAPANESE:

1. Where is the post office?

____

____

2. Where are the stairs?

____

____

3. Where is my wallet?

____

____

1. ゆうびん局は、どこですか。
2. かいだんは、どこですか。
3. さいふは、どこですか。

PHRASE 67

日本	へ	は、	いつ	行きます	か。
Nihon	**e**	**wa,**	**itsu**	**ikimasu**	**ka.**
Japan	to	[PART]	when	to go	[QUESTION FORM]

= When are you going to Japan?

COPY THE JAPANESE SENTENCE:

VOCABULARY:

いつ **itsu** = when

薬 **kusuri** = medicine

店 **mise** = store

夏休み **natsu-yasumi** = summer break

▪ **NOTES** ▪

Summer break in Japan is from about mid-July until the end of August. The academic year ends in March and the new academic year starts in early April.

WRITE THE FOLLOWING IN JAPANESE:

1. When is summer break?

2. When are you going to the store?

3. When are you taking the medicine?

1. 夏休みは、いつですか。
2. 店には、いつ行きますか。
3. 薬は、いつ飲みますか。

PHRASE 68

私 は、今日 勉強 を する。

Watashi wa, kyō benkyō o suru.

I [PART] today study [PART] to do [DICTIONARY FORM]

= I will study today.

COPY THE JAPANESE SENTENCE:

VOCABULARY:

ホテル **hoteru** = hotel

自転車 **jitensha** = bicycle

そうじをします **sōji o shimasu** = to clean

おばあさん **obāsan** = grandmother

▪ **NOTES** ▪

The dictionary form (also called the plain form or the informal form) is used in casual speech. You use this form with your family and your friends. On this sheet, we are concentrating on Group 3 verbs (します **shimasu** and 来ます **kimasu**). These are irregular verbs. The dictionary form for します **shimasu** is する **suru,** and for 来ます **kimasu** it is 来る **kuru.**

WRITE THE FOLLOWING IN JAPANESE:

1. My grandmother will come to the hotel today.

2. I will clean the house.

3. My teacher will come to school by bicycle.

1. おばあさんは、今日ホテルへ来る。
2. 私は、うちをそうじする。
3. 先生は、自転車で学校へ来る。

PHRASE 69

私　は、ぶた肉　を　食べる。

Watashi wa, butaniku o taberu.

I [PART] pork [PART] to eat = I will eat pork.

COPY THE JAPANESE SENTENCE:

VOCABULARY:

ぶた肉 **butaniku** = pork

写真 **shashin** = photograph

おじいさん **ojiisan** = grandfather

▪ NOTES ▪

On this page we focus on Group 2 verbs (refer to page viii) in their dictionary る **RU** form. For Group 2 verbs, simply drop the ます **MASU** ending and add る **RU** to get the dictionary form.

WRITE THE FOLLOWING IN JAPANESE:

1. My grandfather will watch TV.

2. I will look at photographs.

3. I will eat at a restaurant.

1. おじいさんは、テレビを見る。
2. 私は、写真を見る。
3. 私は、レストランで食べる。

PHRASE 70

私	は、	今日	イギリス	へ	行く。
Watashi	**wa,**	**kyō**	**Igirisu**	**e**	**iku.**
I	[PART]	today	Great Britain	to	to go

= I will go to Great Britain today.

COPY THE JAPANESE SENTENCE:

VOCABULARY:

イギリス **Igirisu** = Great Britain

消します **keshimasu** = to erase, to put off, to turn off

借ります **karimasu** = to borrow

切ります **kirimasu** = to cut

▪ NOTES ▪

On this page we focus on Group 1 verbs (refer to page viii) in their dictionary る **RU** form. For Group 1 verbs, simply drop the ます **MASU** ending, change the last い **i** to the う **u** sound. For example: 行きます **ikiMASU** → 行き **iki** → 行く **iku**.

WRITE THE FOLLOWING IN JAPANESE:

1. I will borrow a book.

2. I will cut vegetables.

3. I will turn off the TV.

1. 私は、本を借りる。
2. 私は、野菜を切る。
3. 私は、テレビを消す。

PHRASE 71

私　は、日本語　を　教える　のが　好き　です。

Watashi wa, Nihon-go o oshieru no ga suki desu.

I [PART] Japanese [PART] to teach [PART] like [COPULA]

= I like teaching Japanese.

COPY THE JAPANESE SENTENCE:

VOCABULARY:

教えます **oshiemasu** = to teach

さんぽをします **sanpo o shimasu** = to stroll, to go for a walk

外国語 **gaikokugo** = foreign language

山 **yama** = mountain

▪ **NOTES** ▪

On this page, we will learn the phrase: PERSON は **WA** + Dictionary Form + のが好きです **no ga suki desu**. のが **NO GA** changes the verb into a noun and 好き **suki** means "to like."

WRITE THE FOLLOWING IN JAPANESE:

1. My dad likes to go to the mountains.

2. My grandmother likes to take a stroll.

3. My younger sister likes to study foreign languages.

1. 父は、山へ行くのが好きです。
2. おばあさんは、さんぽをするのが好きです。
3. 妹は、外国語を勉強するのが好きです。

PHRASE 72

父　は、歌う　のが　じょうず　です。

Chichi　wa,　utau　no ga　jōzu　desu.

My father [PART] to sing [PART] skillful [COPULA]

= My dad is skillful at singing.

COPY THE JAPANESE SENTENCE:

VOCABULARY:

写真をとります **shashin o torimasu** = to take a picture

ピアノをひきます **piano o hikimasu** = to play the piano

歌います **utaimasu** = to sing

▪ **NOTES** ▪

PERSON は **WA** Dictionary Form のがじょうずです **no ga jōzu desu**. This form is somewhat similar to the previous one on forming nouns from verbs in their dictionary form, except we use のがじょうずです **no ga jōzu desu** for the ending, to express one's skill in doing something.

WRITE THE FOLLOWING IN JAPANESE:

1. My mom is skillful at cooking.

2. My grandfather is skillful at playing the piano.

3. My younger brother is skillful at taking photographs.

1. 母は、料理をするのがじょうずです。
2. おじいさんは、ピアノをひくのがじょうずです。
3. 弟は、写真をとるのがじょうずです。

PHRASE 73

私　は、日本　へ　行く　つもり　です。

Watashi wa, Nihon e iku tsumori desu.

I [PART] Japan to to go plan on [COPULA]

= I am planning to go to Japan.

COPY THE JAPANESE SENTENCE:

VOCABULARY:

つもり **tsumori** = plan, intention

たいしかん **taishikan** = embassy

来週 **raishū** = next week

今晩 **konban** = tonight

たくさん **takusan** = a lot

旅行 **ryokō** = traveling

▪ NOTES ▪

Please refer to Phrase 70 Notes on how to form Group 1 verbs' dictionary form.

WRITE THE FOLLOWING IN JAPANESE:

1. I am planning to go to the embassy tomorrow.

2. I am planning to travel next week.

3. I am planning to study a lot tonight.

1. 私は明日、たいしかんへ行くつもりです。
2. 私は来週、旅行に行くつもりです。
3. 私は今晩、たくさん勉強するつもりです。

PHRASE 74

私　は、き色　の　ほう　が　みどり　より　好きです。

Watashi wa, ki'iro no hō ga midori yori suki desu.

I [PART] yellow [PART] alternate [PART] green more than like [COPULA]

= I like yellow more than green.

COPY THE JAPANESE SENTENCE:

VOCABULARY:

しょうゆ **shōyu** = soy sauce

塩 **shio** = salt

き色 **ki'iro** = yellow (color)

みどり **midori** = green (color)

オートバイ **ōtobai** = motorcycle

▪ NOTES ▪

Here, we introduce のほうが **no hō ga** to make comparisons, with より **yori** "more". The sentence can simply be: PERSON は **WA** SUBJECT #1 のほうが **no hō ga** SUBJECT #2 より好きです **yori suki desu**.

WRITE THE FOLLOWING IN JAPANESE:

1. I like newspapers more than magazines.

2. I like cars more than motorcycles.

3. I like soy sauce more than salt.

1. 私は、新聞のほうがざっしより好きです。
2. 私は、車のほうがオートバイより好きです。
3. 私は、しょうゆのほうが塩より好きです。

PHRASE 75

私　は、動物　の　中　で　犬　が　一番　好きです。

Watashi wa, dōbutsu no naka de inu ga ichiban suki desu.

I [PART] animal [PART] among [PART] dog [PART] most like [COPULA]

= I like dogs the most among all animals.

COPY THE JAPANESE SENTENCE:

VOCABULARY:

国 **kuni** = country

ゴルフ **gorufu** = golf

動物 **dōbutsu** = animals

中で **naka de** = among

ぶどう **budō** = grapes

スポーツ **supōtsu** = sports

果物 **kudamono** = fruit

▪ **NOTES** ▪

いちばん好きです **Ichiban suki desu** — this is to denote "the most/most liked" idea.

WRITE THE FOLLOWING IN JAPANESE:

1. Among sports, I like golf the most.

2. Among fruits, I like grapes the most.

3. Among countries, I like Japan the most.

1. 私は、スポーツの中でゴルフが一番好きです。
2. 私は、果物の中でぶどうが一番好きです。
3. 私は、国の中で日本が一番好きです。

PHRASE 76

だんだん　寒く　なりました。

Dandan　samuku　narimashita.

Gradually　cold　became　=　It has gradually become colder.

COPY THE JAPANESE SENTENCE:

VOCABULARY:

だんだん **dandan** = gradually

寒い **samui** = is cold

甘い **amai** = is sweet

なります **narimasu** = to become

明るい **akarui** = is bright

さとう **satō** = sugar

▪ NOTES ▪

Many people who travel to Japan will notice that Japanese sweets are usually not as sweet as in the U.S. The portion sizes are smaller and most places do not offer refills for their drinks. On this page, we learn to form adverbs: to form an adverb from a な **NA** adjective, simply add に **ni** to a な **NA** adjective. For い **I** adjectives, drop the い **i** ending and add く **ku** to from an adverb.

WRITE THE FOLLOWING IN JAPANESE:

1. It has gradually become brighter.

____

____

2. With the sugar, it has become sweeter.

____

____

3. The dog has become bigger.

____

____

1. だんだん明るくなりました。
2. さとうで甘くなりました。
3. 犬は大きくなりました。

PHRASE 77

私　は、　日本語　を　勉強　した。

Watashi wa, Nihon-go o benkyō shita.

I [PART] Japanese language [PART] study did [DICTIONARY FORM]

= I studied Japanese language.

COPY THE JAPANESE SENTENCE:

VOCABULARY:

逃げます **nigemasu** = to escape

入院します **nyūin shimasu** = to be hospitalized

入学します **nyūgaku shimasu** = to enter school

今年 **kotoshi** = this year

▪ NOTES ▪

In order to create the informal past tense, you will need to first convert the verb to the て **TE** form and then change the て **te** to た **ta** (eg. 行って **itte** → 行った **itta**; 食べて **tabete** → 食べた **tabeta**).

WRITE THE FOLLOWING IN JAPANESE:

1. I entered college this year.

2. The dog escaped yesterday.

3. My grandmother was hospitalized.

1. 私は、今年大学に入学した。
2. 昨日、犬は逃げた。
3. おばあさんは、入院した。

PHRASE 78

私　は、日本　へ　行った　こと　が　あります。

Watashi	**wa,**	**Nihon**	**e**	**itta**	**koto**	**ga**	**arimasu.**
I	[PART]	Japan	to	went	experience	[PART]	there is

= I have been to Japan.

COPY THE JAPANESE SENTENCE:

VOCABULARY:

ことがあります **koto ga arimasu** = have the experience

引っこします **hikkoshimasu** = to move (house)

集めます **atsumemasu** = to collect something

送ります **okurimasu** = to send (a thing), to dispatch

かざります **kazarimasu** = to decorate

▪ NOTES ▪

Did you know that Pokemon originally came from Japan? You will see a lot of reference to Japan in the shows as well as the goods they sell.

WRITE THE FOLLOWING IN JAPANESE:

1. I have decorated using flowers.

2. I have sent a letter.

3. I have moved house.

1. 私は、花をかざったことがあります
2. 私は、手紙を送ったことがあります。
3. 私は、引っこしたことがあります。

PHRASE 79

早く 起きた ら、 運動 します。

Hayaku okita ra, undō shimasu.

Early wake up if, exercise to do

= If I wake up early, I will exercise

COPY THE JAPANESE SENTENCE:

VOCABULARY:

早く **hayaku** = early

運動します **undō shimasu** = to exercise

おでん **oden** = Japanese food with fish cakes, daikon and other vegetables

覚えます **oboemasu** = to memorize

体 **karada** = body

出かけます **dekakemasu** = to go out

温かい **atatakai** = is hot

▪ NOTES ▪

Oden is eaten mainly in the winter when it is cold, but it is also enjoyed throughout the year. It is one of those dishes that taste better the longer it sits in the broth. You can find some restaurants that specialize in *oden*, of which some are several generations old.

WRITE THE FOLLOWING IN JAPANESE:

1. If I eat oden, my body will become warm.

2. If I go out, it will be fun.

3. If I memorize Japanese (language), I will be happy.

1. おでんを食べたら、体が温かくなります。
2. 出かけたら、楽しいです。
3. 日本語を覚えたら、うれしいです。

PHRASE 80

この 映画 を 見た こと が ありません。

Kono eiga o mita koto ga arimasen.

This movie [PART] watched experience [PART] there is not

= I have never seen this movie.

COPY THE JAPANESE SENTENCE:

VOCABULARY:

ふぐ **fugu** = blowfish

コンビニ **konbini** = convenience store

神社 **jinja** = shrine

回転ずし **kaitenzushi** = conveyor-belt sushi bar

▪ NOTES ▪

In Japan, you will find conveyor-belt sushi bars. You grab the dish that you like. At the end of a meal, the waiter or waitress will count the number of plates. The plates are color coded and the price of each item is based on the color or design of the plate.

WRITE THE FOLLOWING IN JAPANESE:

1. I have never been to a conveyor-belt sushi bar.

2. I have never eaten blowfish.

3. I have never been to a shrine.

1. 私は、回転ずしに行ったことがありません。
2. 私は、ふぐを食べたことがありません。
3. 私は、神社へ行ったことがありません。

PHRASE 81

私 は、ダンス を しない。

Watashi wa, dansu o shinai.

I [PART] dance [PART] do not = I do not dance.

COPY THE JAPANESE SENTENCE:

VOCABULARY:

アナウンサー **anaunsā** = announcer

フィリピン **Firipin** = the Philippines

放送します **hōsō shimasu** = to broadcast

▪ NOTES ▪

The informal negative forms for Group 3 verbs are: しない **shinai** for します **shimasu**, and 来ない **konai** for 来ます **kimasu**.

WRITE THE FOLLOWING IN JAPANESE:

1. My friend will not come from the Philippines.

____

____

2. The announcer will not broadcast.

____

____

3. I will not cook.

____

____

1. 私の友だちは、フィリピンから来ない。
2. アナウンサーは、放送しない。
3. 私は、料理をしない。

PHRASE 82

私　は、魚　を　食べない。

Watashi wa, sakana o tabenai.

I [PART] fish [PART] not eat = I do not eat fish.

COPY THE JAPANESE SENTENCE:

VOCABULARY:

こうどう **kōdō** = auditorium

郊外 **kōgai** = outskirts

研究室 **kenkyūshitsu** = study room/lab

ビデオ **bideo** = video

▪ **NOTES** ▪

In order to form the negative form of any Group 2 verbs, drop off the ます **MASU** ending and then add ない **nai**. For example, 食べます **TABEmasu**: 食べ **TABE** + ない **NAI** = 食べない **TABENAI**.

WRITE THE FOLLOWING IN JAPANESE:

1. I do not watch videos in the auditorium.

2. I do not go to the outskirts.

3. I am not at the lab.

1. 私は、こうどうでビデオを見ない。
2. 私は、郊外へ出かけない。
3. 私は、研究室にいない。

PHRASE 83

私　は、本　を　書かない。

Watashi wa, hon o kakanai.

I [PART] book [PART] not write = I will not write a book.

COPY THE JAPANESE SENTENCE:

VOCABULARY:

ぼく **boku** = I (for males)

足 **ashi** = feet

ふみます **fumimasu** = to step on

増えます **fuemasu** = to increase

分かります **wakarimasu** = to understand

▪ NOTES ▪

To form the negative form of any Group 1 verbs, drop off the う **U** ending from the dictionary form, and change the last character of the verb to the /あ **a**/ sound of the hiragana column (page v), then add ない **NAI**. If in step 2 the character is あ **a**, then change to わ **wa**. (E.g., the informal negative of 買います **kaimasu** is 買わない **kawanai**.)

WRITE THE FOLLOWING IN JAPANESE:

1. I do not understand Japanese (language).

2. I will not step on your feet.

3. My money will not increase.

1. ぼくは、日本語が分からない。
2. 私は、足をふまない。
3. 私のお金は、増えない。

PHRASE 84

私　は、今日　学校　へ　行かなくちゃ　いけない。

Watashi wa, kyō gakkō e ikanakucha ikenai.

I [PART] today school to have to go must

= I have to go to school today.

COPY THE JAPANESE SENTENCE:

VOCABULARY:

アルバイト **arubaito** = part-time job

意見 **iken** = opinion

言います **iimasu** = to say

いなか **inaka** = countryside

▪ NOTES ▪

なくちゃいけない VERB in ない **NAI** form = **Nakucha ikenai** is used to indicate something that needs to be done – in the example sentence, it is to go to school today. Refer to page viii for the ない **NAI** form.

WRITE THE FOLLOWING IN JAPANESE:

1. I have to go to my part-time job today.

2. I have to say my opinion.

3. I have to go to the countryside.

1. 私は、アルバイトに行かなくちゃいけない。
2. 私は、意見を言わなくちゃいけないで。
3. 私は、いなかへ行かなくちゃいけない。

PHRASE 85

明日　は、晴れ　でしょう。

Ashita　wa,　hare　deshō.

Tomorrow [PART]　sunny　probably　=　Tomorrow will probably be sunny.

COPY THE JAPANESE SENTENCE:

VOCABULARY:

あなた **anata** = you

ぬれます **nuremasu** = to get wet

くもります **kumorimasu** = cloudy

雪 **yuki** = snow

雨 **ame** = rain

▪ **NOTES** ▪

でしょう **DESHŌ** is added to any noun or adjective in the informal form to mean "probably."

WRITE THE FOLLOWING IN JAPANESE:

1. It will probably snow tomorrow.

2. You will probably get wet in the rain.

3. It will gradually be cloudy.

1. 明日は、雪でしょう。
2. あなたは、雨でぬれるでしょう。
3. だんだん、くもるでしょう。

PHRASE 86

牛乳 を 飲まない で ください。

Gyūnyū o nomanai de kudasai.

Milk [PART] not drink [PART] please = Please do not drink milk.

COPY THE JAPANESE SENTENCE:

VOCABULARY:

いじめます **ijimemasu** = to tease

動きます **ugokimasu** = to move

牛乳 **gyūnyū** = milk

えんりょします **enryo shimasu** = to be reserved/restrained, to hold back

▪ NOTES ▪

Verb-ない **NAI** (informal) + ください **KUDASAI** expressions are used to request someone not to do something.

WRITE THE FOLLOWING IN JAPANESE:

1. Please do not move.

2. Please do not hold back (that is, be free)

3. Please do not tease.

1. 動かないでください。
2. えんりょしないでください。
3. いじめないでください。

PHRASE 87

食べる 前 に、手 を 洗って ください。

Taberu mae ni, te o aratte kudasai.

To eat before [PART] hand [PART] wash please

= Please wash your hands before eating.

COPY THE JAPANESE SENTENCE:

VOCABULARY:

洗います **araimasu** = to wash

前に **mae ni** = before

ズボン **zubon** = trousers

走ります **hashirimasu** = to run

出かけます **dekakemasu** = to go out

はきます **hakimasu** = to wear (below the waist)

じゅんびします **junbi shimasu** = to prepare

▪ NOTES ▪

In Japanese, there are various verbs for "to wear," depending on the parts of body the item is used. Here, we use はきます **hakimasu** for pants and shorts.

WRITE THE FOLLOWING IN JAPANESE:

1. Please wear your pants before going out.

2. Please prepare before going to Japan.

3. Please run before you sleep.

1. 出かける前に、ズボンをはいてください。
2. 日本へ行く前に、じゅんびしてください。
3. ねる前に、走ってください。

PHRASE 88

おすし は おいしい ので、たくさん ちゅうもん します。

O-sushi	**wa,**	**oishii**	**no de,**	**takusan**	**chūmon**	**shimasu.**
Sushi	[PART]	delicious	so	a lot	order	to do

= Sushi is delicious so I will order a lot of it.

COPY THE JAPANESE SENTENCE:

VOCABULARY:

ちゅうもん **chūmon** = order

病院 **byōin** = hospital

病気(の) **byōki (no)** = is sick

つまらない **tsumaranai** = is boring

かぜをひきます **kaze o hikimasu** = to catch a cold

薬を飲みます **kusuri o nomimasu** = to take medicine

▪ NOTES ▪

Here, we use ので **NO DE** to indicate a reason for something, like ordering a lot of sushi. The ので **NO DE** is attached to nouns and adjectives in the informal form. For な **Na** adjectives you will need to attach a な **NA** before adding ので **NO DE**.

WRITE THE FOLLOWING IN JAPANESE:

1. I am sick so I will go to the hospital.

____

____

2. The movie is boring so I will go home.

____

____

3. I caught a cold so I will take medicine.

____

____

1. 私は、病気なので、病院へ行きます。
2. 映画がつまらないので、帰ります。
3. かぜをひいたので、薬を飲みます。

PHRASE 89

私　は、　母　から　ゆびわ　を　もらいました。

Watashi wa, haha kara yubiwa o moraimashita.

I [PART] my mom from ring [PART] received

= I received a ring from my mom.

COPY THE JAPANESE SENTENCE:

VOCABULARY:

ゆびわ **yubiwa** = ring

もらいます **moraimasu** = to receive

ペット **petto** = a pet

ぼうし **bōshi** = hat

▪ NOTES ▪

For the next few pages the sentence structure will focus on giving and receiving. Remember this sentence structure: Receiver は **WA** Giver に **NI**/から **KARA** Object を **O** もらいます **moraimasu**.

WRITE THE FOLLOWING IN JAPANESE:

1. My mom received a pet from my dad.

____

____

2. I received a hat from my friend.

____

____

3. I received money from my grandmother.

____

____

1. 母は、父からペットをもらいました。
2. 私は、友だちからぼうしをもらいました。
3. 私は、おばあさんからお金をもらいました。

PHRASE 90

私　は　校長先生　に、花びん　を　さしあげました。

Watashi wa kōchō-sensei ni, kabin o sashiagemashita.

I [PART] school principal [PART] vase [PART] gave [HUMBLE FORM]

= I gave the school principal a vase.

COPY THE JAPANESE SENTENCE:

VOCABULARY:

校長先生 **kōchō-sensei** = school principal

花びん **kabin** = vase

お酒 **o-sake** = alcohol, rice wine

かさ **kasa** = umbrella

▪ NOTES ▪

The normal word for "to give" is あげます **agemasu**. However, in Japanese, different words will be used for the same meaning when there is hierarchy/status involved. For example, さしあげます **sashi-gemasu** is used when the receiver is of "a higher status" than the giver (and when both people are not in the same family). You will use あげます **agemasu** when you gave a present to a friend.

WRITE THE FOLLOWING IN JAPANESE:

1. I will give the teacher sweets.

2. I will give my friend's mom an umbrella.

3. I will give my friend's dad rice wine.

1. 私は先生に、おかしをさしあげます。
2. 私は友だちのお母さんに、かさをさしあげます。
3. 私は友だちのお父さんに、お酒をさしあげます。

PHRASE 91

友だち は、 私 に 食べ物 を くれました。

Tomodachi wa, watashi ni tabemono o kuremashita.

Friend [PART] I [PART] food [PART] gave

= A friend gave me food.

COPY THE JAPANESE SENTENCE:

VOCABULARY:

テーブル **tēburu** = table

社長 **shachō** = company president

灰皿 **haizara** = ashtray

バター **batā** = butter

くれます **kuremasu** = to give to me/my family

▪ **NOTES** ▪

This sentence structure symbolizes the "in" versus "out" culture of Japan. In this sentence structure, the giver is an outsider and the receiver must be a family member. The receiver can also be "I" and the giver in that case can be anyone.

WRITE THE FOLLOWING IN JAPANESE:

1. My friend gave me an ashtray.

____

____

2. My mom gave me butter.

____

____

3. The company president gave my dad a table.

____

____

1. 友だちは、私に灰皿をくれました。
2. 母は、私にバターをくれました。
3. 社長は、父にテーブルをくれました。

PHRASE 92

父 は、 医者 です。

Chichi wa, isha desu.

My dad [PART] medical doctor [COPULA] = My dad is a medical doctor.

COPY THE JAPANESE SENTENCE:

VOCABULARY:

医者 **isha** = medical doctor

べんごし **bengoshi** = lawyer

主婦 **shufu** = homemaker

かんごし **kangoshi** = nurse

▪ NOTES ▪

As times change, words have evolved, especially for certain jobs. The word for nurse was かんごふ **kangofu** but most people now use the word かんごし **kangoshi** to include male nurses. The kanji for a stay-at-home mother is 主婦 **shufu** and the kanji for a stay-at-home father is 主夫 **shufu**.

WRITE THE FOLLOWING IN JAPANESE:

1. My older sister is a nurse.

____

____

2. My mom is a homemaker.

____

____

3. My younger sister is a lawyer.

____

____

1. 姉は、かんごしです。
2. 母は、主婦です。
3. 妹は、べんごしです。

PHRASE 93

私　は、フォーク　で　ケーキ　を 食べました。

Watashi wa, fōku de kēki o tabemashita.

I [PART] fork [PART] cake [PART] ate

= I ate cake with a fork.

COPY THE JAPANESE SENTENCE:

VOCABULARY:

フォーク **fōku** = fork

スープ **sūpu** = soup

スプーン **supūn** = spoon

ナイフ **naifu** = knife

▪ NOTES ▪

In general, で **DE** is used with a tool to denote "by means of," e.g. フォークで **fōku de** (in the example sentence) means "by means of/with a fork." You can use で **de** with a computer if it is the tool to help you do something.

WRITE THE FOLLOWING IN JAPANESE:

1. I will drink soup with a spoon.

2. I will eat steak with a fork and knife.

3. I will eat sushi with chopsticks.

1. 私は、スプーンでスープを飲みます。
2. 私は、フォークとナイフでステーキを食べます。
3. 私は、おはしでおすしを食べます。

PHRASE 94

私　は、本　が　いります。

Watashi wa, hon ga irimasu.

I [PART] book [PART] need = I need a book.

COPY THE JAPANESE SENTENCE:

VOCABULARY:

いります **irimasu** = to need (informal)

ガイドブック **gaidobukku** = guidebook

ちゃわん **chawan** = rice bowl

かさ **kasa** = umbrella

けしごむ **keshigomu** = eraser

▪ NOTES ▪

In Japan, you will find a police box, 交番 **kōban**, throughout the country. You can seek their help if you need to look for directions, report incidents or when you lose something. The police are very helpful and police boxes very easy to locate.

WRITE THE FOLLOWING IN JAPANESE:

1. I need an umbrella and a guidebook.

____

____

2. I need a rice bowl and chopsticks.

____

____

3. I need a pencil and an eraser.

____

____

1. 私は、かさとガイドブックがいります。
2. 私は、ちゃわんとはしがいります。
3. 私は、えんぴつとけしごむがいります。

PHRASE 95

ボールペン を、貸して ください。

Bōrupen o, kashite kudasai.

Ballpoint pen [PART] to lend please

= Please lend me a ballpoint pen.

COPY THE JAPANESE SENTENCE:

VOCABULARY:

貸します **kashimasu** = to lend

つくえ **tsukue** = desk

ボールペン **bōrupen** = ballpoint pen

かがみ **kagami** = mirror

着物 **kimono** = kimono

▪ NOTES ▪

What is generally referred to as a 着物 **kimono** in English is a ゆかた **yukata**, which is a light-weight cotton piece of clothing, usually worn inhouse. A genuine *kimono* costs a lot and has many layers.

WRITE THE FOLLOWING IN JAPANESE:

1. Please lend me a desk.

2. Please lend me a kimono.

3. Please lend me a mirror.

1. つくえを、貸してください。
2. 着物を、貸してください。
3. かがみを、貸してください。

PHRASE 96

この　食べ物　は、おいしい　です。

Kono　tabemono　wa,　oishii　desu.

This　food　[PART]　delicious　[COPULA]　=　This food is delicious.

COPY THE JAPANESE SENTENCE:

VOCABULARY:

この **kono** = this (noun)

げんかん **genkan** = entry way

洋服 **yōfuku** = western-style clothing

かわいい **kawaii** = is cute

りっぱ **rippa** = is splendid

▪ NOTES ▪

In Japanese houses, you will notice that there is a げんかん **genkan**, or an entry way. Here, you will change from your shoes to either your slippers or just walk around in your socks. You will also often find an umbrella stand here so that you don't bring a wet umbrella into the house.

WRITE THE FOLLOWING IN JAPANESE:

1. This entry way is splendid.

2. This western-style clothing is cute.

3. This flower is pretty.

1. このげんかんは、りっぱです。
2. この洋服は、かわいいです。
3. この花は、きれいです。

PHRASE 97

この　えんぴつ　は、私　の　です。

Kono enpitsu wa, watashi no desu.

This pencil [PART] I [PART] [COPULA] = This pencil is mine.

COPY THE JAPANESE SENTENCE:

VOCABULARY:

私の **watashi no** = mine

スカート **sukāto** = skirt

背広 **sebiro** = business suit

かぎ **kagi** = key

じ書 **jisho** = dictionary

▪ NOTES ▪

The particle の **NO** is used as a possessive marker. It will be helpful to think of it as an "'s." For this sentence structure, it is pretty much the same as the English sentence structure.

WRITE THE FOLLOWING IN JAPANESE:

1. This key is yours.

2. This dictionary is the teacher's.

3. This business suit is mine.

1. このかぎは、あなたのです。
2. このじ書は、先生のです。
3. この背広は、私のです。

PHRASE 98

その　切手　は、私　の　です。

Sono kitte wa, watashi no desu.

That postage stamp [PART] I [PART] [COPULA]

= That postage stamp is mine.

COPY THE JAPANESE SENTENCE:

VOCABULARY:

その **sono** = that (noun)

箱 **hako** = box

切手 **kitte** = postage stamp

切符 **kippu** = ticket

はがき **hagaki** = postcard

▪ NOTES ▪

At a train station, there are ticket machines at the entrance. You can buy a single trip ticket by looking up the network map to find the correct fare, or you can buy a prepaid card like スイカ **Suica** or パスモ **Pasmo**, which allows you to use the card for multiple trips.

WRITE THE FOLLOWING IN JAPANESE:

1. That ticket is my mom's.

2. That box is my dad's.

3. That postcard is my younger brother's.

1. その切符は、母のです。
2. その箱は、父のです。
3. そのはがきは、弟のです。

PHRASE 99

この 魚 を、食べて みます。

Kono sakana o, tabete mimasu.

This fish [PART] eat try = I will try this fish.

COPY THE JAPANESE SENTENCE:

VOCABULARY:

サンドイッチ **sandoicchi** = sandwich

スカーフ **sukāfu** = scarf

建物 **tabemono** = building

色 **iro** = color

ぬります **nurimasu** = to paint

▪ NOTES ▪

みます **Mimasu** in this sentence means "to try"and therefore it is written in hiragana rather than in kanji. The form VERB-て **TE** + みます **MIMASU** is used to say "try to … ."

WRITE THE FOLLOWING IN JAPANESE:

1. I will try to buy a scarf.

2. I will try to go to this building.

3. I will try to paint in this color.

1. スカーフを、買ってみます。
2. この建物へ、行ってみます。
3. この色で、ぬってみます。

PHRASE 100

私　は、シャツ　を　着ます。

Watashi wa, shatsu o kimasu.

I [PART] shirt [PART] to wear = I wear a shirt.

COPY THE JAPANESE SENTENCE:

VOCABULARY:

着ます **kimasu** = to wear (above the waist)

シャツ **shatsu** = shirt

ブラウス **burausu** = blouse

ジャケット **jaketto** = jacket

▪ NOTES ▪

In Japanese, there are several ways to say "to wear." Previously in Phrase 89 we learned to use はきます **hakimasu** with pants and shorts. Here, we learn to use 着ます **kimasu** "to wear" with items of clothing worn above the waist.

WRITE THE FOLLOWING IN JAPANESE:

1. I will wear a jacket.

2. My mom will wear a blouse.

3. My dad wore a shirt.

1. 私は、ジャケットを着ます。
2. 母は、ブラウスを着ます。
3. 父は、シャツを着ました。

PHRASE 101

父 は、ショートパンツ を はいています。

Chichi wa, shōtopantsu o haiteimasu.

My dad [PART] shorts [PART] wearing

= My dad is wearing shorts.

COPY THE JAPANESE SENTENCE:

VOCABULARY:

はきます **hakimasu** = to wear (below the waist)

ショートパンツ **shōtopantsu** = shorts

下着 **shitagi** = underwear

パンツ **pantsu** = pants, underwear

▪ NOTES ▪

You previously learned the word, ズボン **zubon** for pants or trousers. Here, you learn another word パンツ **PANTSU** – a loanword – for pants or underwear. This word is preferred by younger people.

WRITE THE FOLLOWING IN JAPANESE:

1. My dad is wearing pants.

____

____

2. My younger brother is wearing underwear.

____

____

3. My mom is wearing socks.

____

____

1. 父は、パンツをはいています。
2. 弟は、下着をはいています。
3. 母は、くつ下をはいています。

PHRASE 102

私　は、ぼうし　を　かぶっています。

Watashi wa, bōshi o kabutteimasu.

I [PART] hat [PART] wearing = I am wearing a hat.

COPY THE JAPANESE SENTENCE:

VOCABULARY:

かぶっています **kabutteimasu** = is wearing (on your head)

あかい **akai** = is red

かつら **katsura** = wig

かっこいい **kakkoii** = is stylish

▪ NOTES ▪

You will notice in Japan quite a few ladies carry sun umbrellas or wear hats when outdoors – this is to avoid the sun.

WRITE THE FOLLOWING IN JAPANESE:

1. I am wearing a red hat.

2. My grandmother is wearing a wig.

3. My older brother is wearing a stylish hat.

1. 私は、あかいぼうしをかぶっています。
2. おばあちゃんは、かつらをかぶっています。
3. 兄は、かっこいいぼうしをかぶっています。

PHRASE 103

明日　は、学校　が　ない　かも　しれない　です。

Ashita wa, gakkō ga nai kamo shirenai desu.

Tomorrow [PART] school [PART] none probably [COPULA]

= There probably won't be school tomorrow.

COPY THE JAPANESE SENTENCE:

VOCABULARY:

かも　しれない **kamo shirenai** = probably

風 **kaze** = wind

吹きます **fukimasu** = to blow

こわれます **kowaremasu** = to break

泊まります **tomarimasu** = to stay

▪ NOTES ▪

In Japanese, most of the important information like "not" and "probably" are at the end of the sentence. "Not" or "probably" is considered part of a verb, and hence one gets to know the meaning of a sentence based on the endings of a sentence. かもしれない **kamo shirenai** can be used to indicate a possibility of something happening.

WRITE THE FOLLOWING IN JAPANESE:

1. It will probably break.

____

____

2. The wind will probably blow tomorrow.

____

____

3. My mom will probably stay.

____

____

1. こわれるかもしれないです。
2. 明日は、風が吹くかもしれないです。
3. 母は、泊まるかもしれないです。

PHRASE 104

この おすし は、おいしい し、新せん です。

Kono o-sushi wa, oishii shi, shinsen desu.

This sushi [PART] delicious and fresh [COPULA]

= This sushi is delicious and fresh.

COPY THE JAPANESE SENTENCE:

____

____

____

VOCABULARY:

新せん **shinsen** = is fresh

古い **furui** = is old (not for people)

かわいい **kawaii** = is cute

やさしい **yasashii** = is nice

きたない **kitanai** = is dirty

えいようがあります **eiyō ga arimasu** = substantial

▪ NOTES ▪

In Japanese, here are two different words for the idea of "old": ふるい **furui** is used for inanimate things (books, etc.), and としをとっています **toshi o totteimasu** for people getting old.

WRITE THE FOLLOWING IN JAPANESE:

1. The dog is cute and nice.

2. My house is dirty and old.

3. The fresh vegetables are delicious and substantial.

1. 犬はかわいいし、やさしいです。
2. うちはきたないし、古いです。
3. 新せんな野菜はおいしいし、えいようがあります。

PHRASE 105

野菜 を 食べ たら どう ですか。

Yasai o tabe tara dō desu ka.

Vegetables [PART] eat if how [COPULA QUESTION]

= How about eating some vegetables?

COPY THE JAPANESE SENTENCE:

VOCABULARY:

どう **dō** = how (about)

スキー **sukī** = ski

手伝います **tetsudaimasu** = to help out

電話をかけます **denwa o kakemasu** = to call on the phone

訪問します **hōmon shimasu** = to visit

▪ NOTES ▪

This sentence structure たらどう **TARA DŌ** is a great way to suggest something to someone politely.

WRITE THE FOLLOWING IN JAPANESE:

1. How about visiting your grandmother?

____

____

2. How about calling your father?

____

____

3. How about skiing?

____

____

1. おばあさんを訪問したらどうですか。
2. おとうさんに電話をかけたらどうですか。
3. スキーをしたらどうですか。

PHRASE 106

私　は、　出版社　で　働いています。

Watashi wa, shuppan-sha de hataraiteimasu.

I [PART] publishing company [PART] working

= I am working in a publishing company.

COPY THE JAPANESE SENTENCE:

VOCABULARY:

働いています **hataraiteimasu** = working

出版社 **shuppan-sha** = publishing company

工場 **kōjō** = factory

おばさん **obasan** = (my) aunt

▪ NOTES ▪

In Japan, it is still a very male-dominated workplace, although it is changing bit by bit. Japanese workers also tend to stay in one company much longer, compared to employees in the United States. You will often see people stay with the same company until their retirement.

WRITE THE FOLLOWING IN JAPANESE:

1. I work in a factory.

2. My aunt works in a college.

3. I work in a school.

1. 私は、工場で働いています。
2. おばさんは、大学で働いています。
3. 私は、学校で働いています。

PHRASE 107

私　は、ラーメン屋　で　バイト していますす。

Watashi wa, rāmenya de baito shiteimasu.

I [PART] ramen restaurant [PART] part time job doing

= I am working part-time at a ramen restaurant.

COPY THE JAPANESE SENTENCE:

VOCABULARY:

バイトしています **baito shiteimasu** = working part-time

ラーメン屋 **rāmenya** = ramen restaurant

八百屋 **yaoya** = vegetable store

スーパー **sūpā** = supermarket

▪ NOTES ▪

In Japan, there are different types of restaurants specializing in different types of food. You may often find an entire street of ramen restaurants that you are able to choose from. Other restaurants include sushi bars, tonkatsu restaurants, and tempura restaurants.

WRITE THE FOLLOWING IN JAPANESE:

1. I am working part-time at a vegetable shop.

2. I am working part-time at a supermarket.

3. I am working part-time at a department store.

1. 私は、八百屋でバイトしています。
2. 私は、スーパーでバイトしています。
3. 私は、デパートでバイトしています。

PHRASE 108

しゃぶしゃぶ　の　作り方　を、教えてください。

Shabushabu no tsukurikata o oshiete kudasai.

Japanese hotpot dish [PART] how to make [PART] teach please

= Please teach me how to make shabushabu.

COPY THE JAPANESE SENTENCE:

VOCABULARY:

仕方／〜方 **shikata/~kata** = how to

しゃぶしゃぶ **shabushabu** = Japanese hotpot dish

運転 **unten** = driving

教える **oshieru** = to teach, to tell

▪ NOTES ▪

方 **Kata** means "way, method; how to." So to make a "how-to" verb drop the ます **MASU** from a verb in its regular form and add 方 **kata** to it.

WRITE THE FOLLOWING IN JAPANESE:

1. Please teach me how to drive.

2. Please teach me how to use chopsticks.

3. Please teach me how to go to school.

1. 運転の仕方を、教えてください。
2. おはしの使い方を、教えてください。
3. 学校への行き方を、教えてください。

PHRASE 109

テレビは、テーブル　の　上　に　あります。

Terebi	**wa,**	**tēburu**	**no**	**ue**	**ni**	**arimasu.**
TV	[PART]	table	[PART]	top	[PART]	there is

= The TV is on the table.

COPY THE JAPANESE SENTENCE:

VOCABULARY:

上 **ue** = above, top

万年ひつ **man'nenhitsu** = fountain pen

橋 **hashi** = bridge

▪ NOTES ▪

Use の **NO** + PREPOSITION to give the location of an item, e.g. テーブルの上 **tēburu no ue** means "on the table."

WRITE THE FOLLOWING IN JAPANESE:

1. The butter is on the table.

2. The dog is above the bridge.

3. The fountain pen is on the desk.

1. バターは、テーブルの上にあります。
2. 犬は、橋の上にいます。
3. 万年ひつは、つくえの上にあります。

PHRASE 110

荷物 は、かがみ の 左 に あります。

Nimotsu wa, kagami no hidari ni arimasu.

Luggage [PART] mirror [PART] left [PART] there is

= The luggage is to the left of the mirror.

COPY THE JAPANESE SENTENCE:

VOCABULARY:

左 **hidari** = left

かがみ **kagami** = mirror

いす **isu** = chair

荷物 **nimotsu** = luggage

押入れ **oshiire** = closet

▪ NOTES ▪

Japanese-style closets have sliding doors. In traditional houses, the family put the ふとん **futon** (quilted mattress) in the closet. These closets are quite roomy and can be used for different purposes.

WRITE THE FOLLOWING IN JAPANESE:

1. The closet is to the left of the door.

2. The TV is to the left of the chair.

3. The photo is to the left of the desk.

1. 押入れは、ドアの左にあります。
2. テレビは、いすの左にあります。
3. 写真は、つくえの左にあります。

PHRASE 111

畳　は、テーブル　の　よこ　に　あります。

Tatami wa, tēburu no yoko ni arimasu.

Japanese straw mat [PART] table [PART] next to [PART] there is

= The Japanese straw mat is next to the table.

COPY THE JAPANESE SENTENCE:

VOCABULARY:

よこ **yoko** = next to, beside

畳 **tatami** = Japanese straw mat

下 **shita** = below, under

たな **tana** = shelves

▪ NOTES ▪

Traditional Japanese rooms have tatami mats in the room. You will also find tatami in the tea ceremony rooms. You will need to ensure you are not wearing shoes or slippers on the tatami mats so as not to damage the valuable mats.

WRITE THE FOLLOWING IN JAPANESE:

1. The shelves are next to the painting.

2. The suitcase is next to the bed.

3. The wallet is next to the TV.

1. たなは、絵のよこにあります。
2. スーツケースは、ベッドのよこにあります。
3. さいふは、テレビのよこにあります。

PHRASE 112

レストラン は、空港 の 中 に あります。

Resutoran wa, kūkō no naka ni arimasu.

Restaurant [PART] airport [PART] inside [PART] there is

= The restaurant is inside the airport.

COPY THE JAPANESE SENTENCE:

VOCABULARY:

中 **naka** = inside

空港 **kūkō** = airport

図書館 **toshokan** = library

小説 **shōsetsu** = novel

寺 **tera** = temple

▪ NOTES ▪

One of the greatest places to go visiting when in Japan is a temple. You will see temples throughout the country and you will sense the peace within. With careful planning, you may be able to participate in some of the traditional events held at such temples.

WRITE THE FOLLOWING IN JAPANESE:

1. The photo is inside the temple.

2. The key is inside the car.

3. The novel is inside the library.

1. 写真は、寺の中にあります。
2. かぎは、車の中にあります。
3. 小説は、図書館の中にあります。

PHRASE 113

私　は、時々　牛乳　を　飲みます。

Watashi wa, tokidoki gyūnyū o nomimasu.

I [PART] sometimes milk [PART] to drink

= I sometimes drink milk.

COPY THE JAPANESE SENTENCE:

VOCABULARY:

時々 **tokidoki** = sometimes

公園 **kōen** = park

動物園 **dōbutsuen** = zoo

みそしる **misoshiru** = miso soup

▪ NOTES ▪

If you ever have the chance to go to Tokyo and you love zoos, you probably would want to visit the Ueno Zoo. This is one of the biggest zoos in Japan. It is also situated near many museums as well as a park, and is accessed easily by the Yamanote Line.

WRITE THE FOLLOWING IN JAPANESE:

1. I sometimes go to the zoo.

2. I sometimes eat miso soup.

3. I sometimes go to the park.

1. 私は、時々動物園へ行きます。
2. 私は、時々みそしるを飲みます。
3. 私は、時々公園へ行きます。

PHRASE 114

私　は、たいてい　朝ご飯　に　たまご　を　食べます。

Watashi wa, taitei asa-gohan ni tamago o tabemasu.

I [PART] usually breakfast [PART] egg [PART] to eat

= I usually eat eggs for breakfast.

COPY THE JAPANESE SENTENCE:

VOCABULARY:

たいてい **taitei** = usually

ワイン **wain** = wine

やき肉 **yakiniku** = grilled meat Korean-style

ローマ **Rōma** = Rome

▪ **NOTES** ▪

"Usually" and "sometimes" are considered non-specific times and hence there is no particle after these words. Specific times, such as 7:00, will have the particle に **NI** following.

WRITE THE FOLLOWING IN JAPANESE:

1. I usually drink wine.

____

____

2. I usually eat Korean-style grilled meat.

____

____

3. I usually go to Rome.

____

____

1. 私は、たいていワインを飲みます。
2. 私は、たいていやき肉を食べます。
3. 私は、たいていローマへ行きます。

PHRASE 115

私　は、毎日　学校　へ　行きます。

Watashi wa, mainichi gakkō e ikimasu.

I [PART] everyday school to to go

= I go to school every day.

COPY THE JAPANESE SENTENCE:

VOCABULARY:

毎日 **mainichi** = every day

サッカーをします **sakkā o shimasu** = to play soccer

きんトレ **kintore** = weight lifting

いとこ **itoko** = cousin

▪ NOTES ▪

In Japanese, words are often truncated, as in きんトレ **kintore**, which comes from きん **kin** = muscles and トレ **tore** = training. Often condensed to three or four syllables, they become easier to say.

WRITE THE FOLLOWING IN JAPANESE:

1. My cousin lifts weights every day.

2. I play soccer every day.

3. I take a stroll every day.

1. いとこは、毎日きんトレをします。
2. 私は、毎日サッカーをします。
3. 私は、毎日さんぽします。

PHRASE 116

私　は、よく　さんぽ　を　します。

Watashi wa, yoku sanpo o shimasu.

I [PART] often stroll [PART] to do = I often take a stroll.

COPY THE JAPANESE SENTENCE:

VOCABULARY:

たこ **tako** = octopus

よく **yoku** = well, often

ジャケット **jaketto** = jacket

ドラマ **dorama** = TV drama

▪ NOTES ▪

Japanese dramas are often watched by many and are also popular in other countries. They usually last only one season, but the same actors appear in new series all the time.

WRITE THE FOLLOWING IN JAPANESE:

1. I watch Japanese dramas often.

2. I often wear a jacket.

3. I often eat octopus.

1. 私は、よくドラマを見ます。
2. 私は、よくジャケットを着ます。
3. 私は、よくたこを食べます。

PHRASE 117

私 は、いつも 宿題 を します。

Watashi wa, itsumo shukudai o shimasu.

I [PART] always homework [PART] to do

= I always do my homework.

COPY THE JAPANESE SENTENCE:

VOCABULARY:

いつも **itsumo** = always

スコットランド **Sukottorando** = Scotland

刺身 **sashimi** = raw fish

のり **nori** = seaweed

▪ NOTES ▪

Sashimi is sliced raw fish without any rice. When there is rice underneath, it is called sushi. All of the different parts of sushi, including the wasabi, ginger, and soy sauce, are used to help preserve the fish so that it does not go bad.

WRITE THE FOLLOWING IN JAPANESE:

1. My mom always eats seaweed.

2. My dad always goes to Scotland.

3. I always eat raw fish.

1. 母は、いつものりを食べます。
2. 父は、いつもスコットランドへ行きます。
3. 私は、いつも刺身を食べます。

PHRASE 118

私　は、友だち　と　一緒　に　日本　へ　行きます。

Watashi wa, tomodachi to issho ni Nihon e ikimasu.

I [PART] friend [PART] together [PART] Japan to to go

= I will go to Japan with my friend.

COPY THE JAPANESE SENTENCE:

VOCABULARY:

と一緒に **to issho ni** = with

庭 **niwa** = garden

飲み屋 **nomiya** = bar

あさくさ **Asakusa** = Asakusa (district in Tokyo)

▪ NOTES ▪

Asakusa is a district in Tokyo, most famous for the **Senso-ji** (Asakusa Kannon Temple) and Asakusa Shrine. It has one of the most fascinating and traditional streets that lead to **Senso-ji** with shops that have been there for centuries. You can spend a couple of hours here shopping, going to the shrine, eating, and looking at the souvenirs.

WRITE THE FOLLOWING IN JAPANESE:

1. I will go to Asakusa with my friend.

2. I will go to the bar with my older brother.

3. I will go to the garden with my mom.

1. 私は、友だちと一緒にあさくさへ行きます。
2. 私は、兄と一緒に飲み屋へ行きます。
3. 私は、母と一緒に庭へ行きます。

PHRASE 119

私 は、 彼女 と 一緒 に 本 を 読みます。

Watashi wa, kanojo to issho ni hon o yomimasu.

I [PART] girlfriend [PART] together [PART] book [PART] to read

= I will read a book with my girlfriend.

COPY THE JAPANESE SENTENCE:

VOCABULARY:

彼女 **kanojo** = girlfriend

彼し **kareshi** = boyfriend

まんが **manga** = comics

友人 **yūjin** = friend

▪ NOTES ▪

You will find huge bookstores in Japan with people reading books and magazines as they stand in the store. At the bookstores, the staff at the counter often ask you, when you buy a book, if you would like to have a cover put on. It might be a good idea to have this done as it will keep the book from any dirt, and the service is complimentary.

WRITE THE FOLLOWING IN JAPANESE:

1. I will read a magazine with my boyfriend.

2. I will read comics with my friend.

3. I will read the newspapers with my girlfriend.

1. 私は、彼と一緒にざっしを読みます。
2. 私は、友人と一緒にまんがを読みます。
3. 私は、彼女と一緒に新聞を読みます。

PHRASE 120

私　は、うち　で　動画　を　見ます。

Watashi wa, uchi de dōga o mimasu.

I [PART] house [PART] internet clips [PART] to watch

= I will watch internet clips at home.

COPY THE JAPANESE SENTENCE:

VOCABULARY:

教室 **kyōshitsu** = classroom

居間 **ima** = living room

コメディー **komedī** = comedy

動画 **dōga** = internet clips

地下室 **chikashitsu** = basement

げき場 **gekijō** = theater

▪ NOTES ▪

You will most likely not see too many basements in the Japanese homes. However, you will see the basement level of stores and the subway systems all over Japan. Because land is at a premium, Japan uses the land very well by building up and building underground.

WRITE THE FOLLOWING IN JAPANESE:

1. I will watch a movie in the classroom.

____

____

2. My dad will watch TV in the basement.

____

____

3. My mom will watch comedy at the theater.

____

____

1. 私は、教室で映画を見ます。
2. 父は、地下室でテレビを見ます。
3. 母は、げき場でコメディーを見ます。

PHRASE 121

私　は、作文　を　書きます。

Watashi wa, sakubun o kakimasu.

I [PART] essay [PART] to write = I will write an essay.

COPY THE JAPANESE SENTENCE:

VOCABULARY:

公務員 **kōmuin** = government worker

消ぼうし **shōbōshi** = firefighter

ほうこく書 **hōkokusho** = report

さっか **sakka** = author

日記 **nikki** = diary, journal

作品 **sakuhin** = a piece of work (book, film, etc.)

▪ NOTES ▪

Occupations like those of a firefighter, police officer and government workers are all considered noble jobs, just like in many other countries.

WRITE THE FOLLOWING IN JAPANESE:

1. The government officer will write a report.

____

____

2. The author will write a new book.

____

____

3. The firefighter will write a journal.

____

____

1. 公務員は、ほうこく書を書きます。
2. さっかは、新しい本を書きます。
3. 消ぼうしは、日記を書きます。

PHRASE 122

私　は、バレーボール　が　にが手　です。

Watashi wa, baēbōru ga nigate desu.

I [PART] volleyball [PART] weak point [COPULA]

= I am weak in volleyball.

COPY THE JAPANESE SENTENCE:

VOCABULARY:

にが手 **nigate** = is weak (at), is bad (in), is difficult to handle

りくじょう **rikujō** = track (and field) event

あみ物 **amimono** = knitting

つり **tsuri** = fishing

▪ NOTES ▪

You can also use にが手 **nigate** to mean that you don't care for something or somebody. You can say that somebody is にが手 **nigate** if that person scares you or you don't quite get along with that person.

WRITE THE FOLLOWING IN JAPANESE:

1. I am poor in knitting.

____

____

2. I am bad in fishing.

____

____

3. I am weak in track.

____

____

1. 私は、あみ物がにが手です。
2. 私は、つりがにが手です。
3. 私は、りくじょうがにが手です。

PHRASE 123

母　は、テニス　が　とても　じょうず　です。

Haha	**wa,**	**tenisu**	**ga**	**totemo**	**jōzu**	**desu.**
My mom	[PART]	tennis	[PART]	very	skillful	[COPULA]

= My mom is very skillful at tennis.

COPY THE JAPANESE SENTENCE:

VOCABULARY:

とても **totemo** = very

フットボール **futtobōru** = football

絵 **e** = painting

バイオリン **baiorin** = violin

▪ NOTES ▪

In Japanese, particles are not used after an adverb as seen in this phrase: とても **totemo**. The speakers tend to exaggerate how much they feel with this phrase.

WRITE THE FOLLOWING IN JAPANESE:

1. My dad is very skillful at painting.

____

____

2. My friend is very good at violin.

____

____

3. My older brother plays football well.

____

____

1. 父は、絵がとてもじょうずです。
2. 私の友だちは、バイオリンがとてもじょうずです。
3. 兄は、フットボールがとてもじょうずです。

PHRASE 124

私　の　友だち　は、バスケ　が、あまりじょうずじゃないです。

Watashi no tomodachi wa, basuke ga amari jōzu janai desu.

I [PART] friend [PART] basketball [PART] not very skillful is not [COPULA]

= My friend is not very skillful at basketball.

COPY THE JAPANESE SENTENCE:

VOCABULARY:

あまり **amari** = not very

むらさき色 **murasaki'iro** = purple

黄色 **ki'iro** = yellow

スケートボード **sukētobōdo** = skateboard

▪ NOTES ▪

To form adverbs with negative meanings, like "not very," a negative ending is needed at the end of the adverb (じゃない **janai**, in our example). This turns "skillful" to "not skillful." バスケ **Basuke** is an abbreviation of バスケットボール **basukettobōru**.

WRITE THE FOLLOWING IN JAPANESE:

1. My cousin does not like purple much.

____

____

2. My aunt does not like yellow much.

____

____

3. My uncle is not very skillful at skateboarding.

____

____

1. いとこは、むらさき色が、あまり好きじゃないです。
2. おばさんは、黄色が、あまり好きじゃないです。
3. おじさんは、スケートボードが、あまりじょうずじゃないです。

PHRASE 125

兄　は、野球　が、全然　じょうず　じゃない　です。

Ani wa, yakyū ga zenzen jōzu janai desu.

My older brother [PART] baseball [PART] not at all skillful is not [COPULA]

= My older brother is not at all skillful at baseball.

COPY THE JAPANESE SENTENCE:

VOCABULARY:

全然 **zenzen** = not at all

さいほう **saihō** = sewing

チェロ **chero** = cello

カラオケ **karaoke** = karaoke

▪ **NOTES** ▪

Although grammatically incorrect, you will hear people say just 全然 **zenzen** with an affirmative ending like 全然大じょうぶ **zenzen daijōbu** meaning it is absolutely fine.

WRITE THE FOLLOWING IN JAPANESE:

1. My grandfather does not like karaoke at all.

2. I am not skillful at cello at all.

3. My grandmother is not at all skillful at sewing.

1. おじいさんは、カラオケが、全然好きじゃないです。
2. 私は、チェロが、全然じょうずじゃないです。
3. おばあさんは、さいほうが、全然じょうずじゃないです。

PHRASE 126

この パーティー は、楽しい です ね。

Kono	**pātī**	**wa,**	**tanoshii**	**desu**	**ne.**
This	party	[PART]	fun	[COPULA]	isn't it

= This party is fun, isn't it?

COPY THE JAPANESE SENTENCE:

VOCABULARY:

ね **ne** = isn't it, don't you agree?

静か **shizuka** = is quiet

平和 **heiwa** = is peaceful

危ない **abunai** = is dangerous

▪ NOTES ▪

Here, we learn the use of ね **NE** — a handy word to use at the end of a sentence. It seeks confirmation or agreement from the listener.

WRITE THE FOLLOWING IN JAPANESE:

1. The dog is quiet, isn't it?

2. Japan is peaceful, isn't it?

3. This car is dangerous, isn't it?

1. この犬は、静かですね。
2. 日本は、平和ですね。
3. この車は、危ないですね。

PHRASE 127

この　食べ物　は、おいしい　です　よ。

Kono tabemono wa, oishii desu yo.

This food [PART] delicious [COPULA] you know

= This food is delicious, you know.

COPY THE JAPANESE SENTENCE:

VOCABULARY:

よ **yo** = you know

つまらない **tsumaranai** = is boring

恥ずかしい **hazukashii** = is embarrassing

きたない **kitanai** = is dirty

▪ NOTES ▪

When you add よ **YO** at the end of a sentence, it makes the statement stronger. For example, if a person is reluctantly eating something or is hesitating, a person who just ate it can say, この食べ物は、おいしいですよ **kono tabemono wa, oishii desu yo** to tell the other person that the food is delicious.

WRITE THE FOLLOWING IN JAPANESE:

1. This is embarrassing, you know.

2. This house is dirty, you know.

3. This game is boring, you know.

1. これは、恥ずかしいですよ。
2. このうちは、きたないですよ。
3. この試合は、つまらないですよ。

PHRASE 128

私　は、午前　七時　ごろ　に　起きます。

Watashi wa, gozen shichi-ji goro ni okimasu.

I [PART] A.M. 7:00 around [PART] to wake up

= I wake up around 7:00 A.M.

COPY THE JAPANESE SENTENCE:

VOCABULARY:

五分前 **go-fun-mae** = five minutes before

五分すぎ **go-fun-sugi** = five minute after

ごろ **goro** = about, around

▪ NOTES ▪

Similar to English, it takes a little bit of practice to get used to saying "5 minutes after/before," "quarter before/after." The word ごろ **goro** is used to show an estimate of the time given. In this section, we go through some of this.

WRITE THE FOLLOWING IN JAPANESE:

1. I will wake up five minutes after 9:00.

____

____

2. I will wake up five minutes before 6:00.

____

____

3. I will wake up at around 6:30.

____

____

1. 私は、九時五分すぎに起きます。
2. 私は、六時五分前に起きます。
3. 私は、六時半ごろに起きます。

PHRASE 129

私　は、午後　十時　に　寝ました。

Watashi wa, gogo jū-ji ni nemashita.

I [PART] P.M. 10:00 [PART] slept = I slept at 10:00 P.M.

COPY THE JAPANESE SENTENCE:

VOCABULARY:

ホテル **hoteru** = hotel

正午 **shōgo** = noon

民宿 **minshuku** = guesthouse, tourist lodging

旅館 **ryokan** = a traditional Japanese inn

着きました **tsukimashita** = to arrive

▪ NOTES ▪

You will see in in the next few pages the differences in the two particles, に **ni** and で **de**. に **Ni** is used after a specific time, and で **de** is used after a place when there's an action word at the end of a sentence.

WRITE THE FOLLOWING IN JAPANESE:

1. I will arrive at 9:00 A.M. at the hotel.

2. I will sleep in a Japanese inn at 11:00 P.M.

3. I arrived at a tourist home at noon.

1. 私は、午前九時にホテルに着きます。
2. 私は、午後十一時に旅館で寝ます。
3. 私は、正午に民宿に着きました。

PHRASE 130

私　は、ギョーザ　を　注文　しました。

Watashi wa, gyōza o chūmon shimashita.

I [PART] potstickers [PART] order did

= I ordered potstickers.

COPY THE JAPANESE SENTENCE:

VOCABULARY:

注文します **chūmon shimasu** = to order

やきそば **yakisoba** = fried noodles

たこやき **takoyaki** = octopus dumpling

ざるそば **zarusoba** = cold buckwheat noodles

▪ NOTES ▪

If you ever have a chance to eat octopus dumplings, they are delicious. The cook will make these in front of you at a stand or you can go to a restaurant where they will bring you the ingredients and you can make them yourself at the table.

WRITE THE FOLLOWING IN JAPANESE:

1. I will order octopus dumplings.

2. I will order fried noodles.

3. I will order cold buckwheat noodles.

1. 私は、たこやきを注文します。
2. 私は、やきそばを注文します。
3. 私は、ざるそばを注文します。

PHRASE 131

私　は、レストラン　で　食事　を　します。

Watashi wa, resutoran de shokuji o shimasu.

I [PART] restaurant [PART] meal [PART] to do

= I will have a meal at a restaurant.

COPY THE JAPANESE SENTENCE:

VOCABULARY:

食事をします **shokuji o shimasu** = to have a meal

きっさ店 **kissaten** = coffee shop

食堂 **shokudō** = dining hall

りょう **ryō** = dorm

▪ NOTES ▪

A lot of people in Japan meet up with their friends at a coffee shop. Usually, an order of drinks does not come with refills, although family restaurants do provide you with an option to order an all-you-can-drink. You will often find the best deals for breakfast at coffee shops where they have special morning sets that include coffee or tea with food for a very reasonable price.

WRITE THE FOLLOWING IN JAPANESE:

1. I will have a meal at the dining hall.

2. I will have a meal at the dorm.

3. I will have a meal at the coffee shop.

1. 私は、食堂で食事をします。
2. 私は、りょうで食事をします。
3. 私は、きっさ店で食事をします。

PHRASE 132

私　は、物理　を　とっています。

Watashi wa, butsuri o totteimasu.

I [PART] physics [PART] is taking = I am taking physics.

COPY THE JAPANESE SENTENCE:

VOCABULARY:

とっています **totteimasu** = is taking

物理 **butsuri** = physics

経済 **keizai** = economics

歴史 **rekishi** = history

▪ NOTES ▪

There are entrance exams that one needs to take for both private and public schools. As you go from one grade to another (elementary to middle school, etc.), you will need to take an entrance exam. When you are applying to colleges, and there are cutoff scores for the admission to a course, you will need to take an exam too.

WRITE THE FOLLOWING IN JAPANESE:

1. I am taking history.

____

____

2. My younger brother is taking economics.

____

____

3. My older brother is taking French (language).

____

____

1. 私は、歴史をとっています。
2. 弟は、経済をとっています。
3. 兄は、フランス語をとっています。

PHRASE 133

私　は、母　を　車　に　乗せて　あげました。

Watashi wa, haha o kuruma ni nosete agemashita.

I [PART] my mom [PART] the car [PART] to put on gave

= I did my mom the favor of giving her a ride in the car.
(I gave my mom a ride in the car.)

COPY THE JAPANESE SENTENCE:

VOCABULARY:

てあげます **te agemasu** = to do someone the favor of

手伝います **tetsudaimasu** = to help

作ります **tsukurimasu** = to make

料理をします **ryōri o shimasu** = to cook

▪ NOTES ▪

The structure here is て **TE** + あげます **AGEMASU**, which means "giving somebody the favor of doing something (for them)."

WRITE THE FOLLOWING IN JAPANESE:

1. I cooked for my friend.

2. I helped my older sister out.

3. I baked a cake for my older brother.

1. 私は、友だちに料理をしてあげました。
2. 私は、姉を手伝ってあげました。
3. 私は、兄にケーキを作ってあげました。

PHRASE 134

私　は、料理　を　作って　もらいました。

Watashi wa, ryōri o tsukutte moraimashita.

I [PART] cooking [PART] to make received

= I received the favor of cooking. (Someone cooked for me.)

COPY THE JAPANESE SENTENCE:

VOCABULARY:

てもらいます **temoraimasu** = to receive the favor of

開けます **akemasu** = to open

閉めます **shimemasu** = to close

つけます **tsukemasu** = to turn on

▪ NOTES ▪

The sentence structure here is て **TE** + もらいます **MORAIMASU** to mean "I will receive the favor of … (= Someone does me a favor)."

WRITE THE FOLLOWING IN JAPANESE:

1. Someone closed the door for me.

2. Someone opened the window for me.

3. Someone turned the TV on for me.

1. 私は、ドアを閉めてもらいました。
2. 私は、窓を開けてもらいました。
3. 私は、テレビをつけてもらいました。

PHRASE 135

母　は、私　に　ケーキ　を　作って　くれました。

Haha wa, watashi ni kēki o tsukutte kuremashita.

My mom [PART] I [PART] cake [PART] to make gave me

= My mom did me the favor of making me a cake. (My mom baked me a cake.)

COPY THE JAPANESE SENTENCE:

VOCABULARY:

てくれます **tekuremasu** = to give to me/my family members

直します **naoshimasu** = to fix

あらいます **araimasu** = to wash

持ちます **mochimasu** = to have, to carry

▪ NOTES ▪

くれます **Kuremasu** is used only when the receiver(s) of an action is me or my family members.

WRITE THE FOLLOWING IN JAPANESE:

1. My dad gave me the favor of washing my car.

____

____

2. My younger brother gave me the favor of fixing the TV.

____

____

3. My friend gave me the favor of carrying some luggages.

____

____

1. 父は、私の車をあらってくれました。
2. 弟は、テレビを直してくれました。
3. 私の友だちは、荷物を持ってくれました。

PHRASE 136

私 は、日本 も フランス も 好き です。

Watashi wa, Nihon mo Furansu mo suki desu.

I [PART] Japan and France also like [COPULA]

= I like both Japan and France.

COPY THE JAPANESE SENTENCE:

VOCABULARY:

タオル **taoru** = towel

化しょう品 **keshōhin** = cosmetics

科学 **kagaku** = science

社会 **shakai** = social studies, society

肉じゃが **nikujaga** = a Japanese dish with beef and potatoes

▪ NOTES ▪

The particle も **MO** is used to mean "both" and "also." In a sentence it is placed between the objects that share the same verb.

WRITE THE FOLLOWING IN JAPANESE:

1. I will eat both Chinese soup noodles and Japanese beef with potatoes.

2. I studied both social studies and science.

3. I bought both cosmetics and a towel.

1. 私は、ラーメンも肉じゃがも食べます。
2. 私は、社会も科学も勉強します。
3. 私は、化しょう品もタオルも買いました。

PHRASE 137

お寿司 は、おいしい し、けんこうにいい です。

O-sushi **wa,** **oishii** **shi** **kenkō ni ii** **desu.**

Sushi [PART] delicious [PART] healthy [COPULA]

= Sushi is not only delicious, but it is also healthy.

COPY THE JAPANESE SENTENCE:

VOCABULARY:

けんこうにいい **kenkō ni ii** = is healthy

やさしい **yasashii** = is nice

感動します **kandō shimasu** = to be moved

温かい **atatakai** = is hot

▪ **NOTES** ▪

The particle し **SHI** is used when you want to stress that something is true not only for X, but also for Y. In this section, we will use it with adjectives (for X and Y), and in the next phrase, we will also use it with verbs.

WRITE THE FOLLOWING IN JAPANESE:

1. This movie is not only interesting, but it is also moving.

____

____

2. My friend is not only nice, but he is also interesting.

____

____

3. Ramen is not only delicious, but it is also hot.

____

____

1. この映画は、おもしろいし、感動します。
2. 私の友だちは、やさしいし、おもしろいです。
3. ラーメンは、おいしいし、温かいです。

PHRASE 138

昨日 は、ケーキ を 作ったし、洗たく も しました。

Kinō wa, kēki o tsukutta shi, sentaku mo shimashita.

Yesterday [PART] cake [PART] make [PART] laundry also did

= Yesterday, I not only made a cake, but I also did the laundry.

COPY THE JAPANESE SENTENCE:

VOCABULARY:

せい理します **seiri shimasu** = to tidy up

さん **san** = suffix for names, Mr./Ms.

かん光します **kankō shimasu** = to tour

会います **aimasu** = to meet

▪ NOTES ▪

In order to use the し **SHI** form with verbs in the middle of a sentence, you will need to have the verbs in the informal form (refer to Phrases 110 and 151). With both adjectives and verbs, し **SHI** has the same meaning of "not only -, but also -."

WRITE THE FOLLOWING IN JAPANESE:

1. Yoko not only toured, but also met up with friends.

2. I not only tidied up, but I also cleaned.

3. I not only shopped, but also played tennis.

1. ようこさんは、かん光したし、友だちにも会いました。
2. 私は、せい理したし、そうじもしました。
3. 私は、買い物したし、テニスもしました。

PHRASE 139

あの	うどん	は、	おいし	そう	です。
Ano	**udon**	**wa,**	**oishi**	**sō**	**desu.**
That over there	Japanese white noodles	[PART]	delicious	looks	[COPULA]

= That Japanese white noodles over there looks delicious.

COPY THE JAPANESE SENTENCE:

____

____

____

VOCABULARY:

ゲーム **gēmu** = game

指わ **yubiwa** = ring

箱 **hako** = box

重い **omoi** = is heavy

▪ NOTES ▪

This section works on い **I** adjectives. The observation is all first-hand and not based solely on what you heard. For い **I** adjectives, you take off the い **i** and add そう **sō.** The **SŌ** form means "it looks like."

WRITE THE FOLLOWING IN JAPANESE:

1. That box over there looks heavy.

2. That ring looks expensive.

3. This game looks fun.

1. あの箱は、重そうです。
2. その指わは、高そうです。
3. このゲームは、楽しそうです。

PHRASE 140

この つくえ は、きれい そう です。

Kono tsukue wa, kirei sō desu.

This desk [PART] clean looks [COPULA] = This desk looks clean.

COPY THE JAPANESE SENTENCE:

VOCABULARY:

有名 **yūmei** = is famous

じゃま **jama** = is a hindrance

子ども **kodomo** = child

大変 **taihen** = is hard, is difficult

▪ NOTES ▪

For な **NA** adjectives, you will just need to add そう **SŌ** to form the "it looks like" structure. Please note that there are several な **NA** adjectives that look like い **I** adjectives: きれい **kirei**, きらい **kirai**, とくい **tokui**, and 有名 **yūmei**.

WRITE THE FOLLOWING IN JAPANESE:

1. The child looks like he's a hindrance.

2. This exam looks difficult.

3. That person looks famous.

1. 子どもは、じゃまそうです。
2. このしけんは、大変そうです。
3. その人は、有名そうです。

PHRASE 141

ハワイ は、あたたかい そう です。

Hawai wa, atatakai sō desu.

Hawaii [PART] warm seems [COPULA] = I heard Hawaii is warm.

COPY THE JAPANESE SENTENCE:

VOCABULARY:

きびしい **kibishii** = is strict

忙しい **isogashii** = is busy

大とうりょう **daitōryō** = president (country)

すばらしい **subarashii** = is wonderful

▪ **NOTES** ▪

This form of そう **SŌ** is also used to imply that what you have heard is from another source, i.e., it is secondhand information.

WRITE THE FOLLOWING IN JAPANESE:

1. I heard the Japanese teacher is strict.

2. I heard the president is busy.

3. I heard the movie is wonderful.

1. 日本語の先生は、きびしいそうです。
2. 大とうりょうは、忙しいそうです。
3. あの映画は、すばらしいそうです。

PHRASE 142

姉　は、日本　へ　行く　そう　です。

Ane	**wa,**	**Nihon**	**e**	**iku**	**sō**	**desu.**
My older sister	[PART]	Japan	to	to go	seems	[COPULA]

= I heard my older sister is going to Japan.

COPY THE JAPANESE SENTENCE:

VOCABULARY:

ゴミを出します **gomi o dashimasu** = to take out the trash

電話をします **denwa o shimasu** = to make a phone call

写真をとります **shashin o torimasu** = to take a picture

店員 **tenin** = shopkeeper

▪ **NOTES** ▪

In order to convert verbs to the "I heard" form, you will need to take off the ます **MASU** and add そう **SŌ** to the verb stem (verb minus ます **masu**).

WRITE THE FOLLOWING IN JAPANESE:

1. I heard the shopkeeper will make a phone call.

____

____

2. I heard the girl will take a picture.

____

____

3. I heard my younger sister will take out the trash.

____

____

1. 店員は、電話をかけるそうです。
2. 女の子は、写真をとるそうです。
3. 妹は、ゴミを出すそうです。

PHRASE 143

この 肉 は、食べ やすい です。

Kono niku wa, tabe yasui desu.

This meat [PART] eat easy [COPULA] = This meat is easy to eat.

COPY THE JAPANESE SENTENCE:

VOCABULARY:

覚えます **oboemasu** = to memorize

登ります **noborimasu** = to climb

かいだん **kaidan** = stairs

薬 **kusuri** = medicine

▪ **NOTES** ▪

The structure VERB-stem + やすい **YASUI** is used to say something is easy to do. You can form it by taking off the ます **MASU** from the verb and adding やすい **yasui.**

WRITE THE FOLLOWING IN JAPANESE:

1. The stairs are easy to climb.

2. This medicine is easy to take.

3. This kanji is easy to memorize.

1. かいだんは、登りやすいです。
2. この薬は、飲みやすいです。
3. この漢字は、覚えやすいです。

PHRASE 144

この 野菜 ジュース は、飲み にくい です。

Kono yasai jūsu wa, nomi nikui desu.

This vegetable juice [PART] drink difficult [COPULA]

= This vegetable juice is hard to drink.

COPY THE JAPANESE SENTENCE:

VOCABULARY:

生物 **seibutsu** = biology

きかい **kikai** = machine

歩きます **arukimasu** = to walk

坂 **saka** = slope

▪ NOTES ▪

Similar to the やすい **-yasui** structure, to say something is difficult to do, use VERB-stem + にくい **-NIKUI**.

WRITE THE FOLLOWING IN JAPANESE:

1. It is difficult to walk on slopes.

2. It is difficult to fix this machine.

3. It is hard to study biology.

1. 坂は、歩きにくいです。
2. このきかいは、直しにくいです。
3. 生物は、勉強しにくいです。

PHRASE 145

さっさと　食べ　なさい。

Sassato　tabe　nasai.

Quickly　eat　[COMMAND]　=　Hurry up and eat!

COPY THE JAPANESE SENTENCE:

VOCABULARY:

片付けます **katazukemasu** = to tidy up

遅れます **okuremasu** = to be late

さっさと **sassato** = quickly

座ります **suwarimasu** = to sit

▪ NOTES ▪

To form this command form, you will need to take off the ます **MASU** from the verb and add なさい **-NASAI**. You will hear this form a lot at schools and when parents talk to their children.

WRITE THE FOLLOWING IN JAPANESE:

1. Quickly tidy up!

____

____

2. Quickly sit here!

____

____

3. You will be late so wake up quickly!

____

____

1. さっさと片付けなさい。
2. さっさとここに座りなさい。
3. 遅れるから、さっさと起きなさい。

PHRASE 146

きのこ を 食べ なくて も いい です。

Kinoko o tabe nakute mo ii desu.

Mushroom [PART] eat not have to [PART] good [COPULA]

= You don't have to eat the mushrooms.

COPY THE JAPANESE SENTENCE:

VOCABULARY:

きのこ **kinoko** = mushroom

帰ります **kaerimasu** = to return

まだ **mada** = not yet

全部 **zenbu** = all

▪ NOTES ▪

To say something needs not be done, use this structure: VERB-stem + ない **NAI** (–い **I**) + くてもいい **kute mo ii.** Remember to change the verbs first, according to their grouping (see page viii).

WRITE THE FOLLOWING IN JAPANESE:

1. You don’t have to return yet.

2. You don’t have to eat it all.

3. You don’t have to study.

1. まだ帰らなくてもいいです。
2. 全部食べなくてもいいです。
3. 勉強しなくてもいいです。

PHRASE 147

ぼく は、ケーキ を 食べて しまいました。

Boku wa, kēki o tabete shimaimashita.

I [PART] cake [PART] eat have done

= I completely ate up the cake.

COPY THE JAPANESE SENTENCE:

VOCABULARY:

こわします **kowashimasu** = to break

ぶつけます **butsukemasu** = to crash

チョコレート **chokorēto** = chocolate

ラップトップ **rapputoppu** = laptop

▪ **NOTES** ▪

The てしまいます **TE SHIMAIMASU** form is created by converting the verb to the て **TE** form and then adding しまいます **shimaimasu**. It means to completely do something with a feeling of regret.

WRITE THE FOLLOWING IN JAPANESE:

1. I finished all of my friend's chocolate.

2. I broke my mom's laptop (regretfully).

3. I crashed my car (regretfully).

1. ともだちのチョコレートを、食べてしまいました。
2. 母のラップトップを、こわしてしまいました。
3. 車を、ぶつけてしまいました。

PHRASE 148

遅くなって しまって すみません。

Osokunatte **shimatte** **sumimasen.**

Being late was sorry = I am sorry to be late.

COPY THE JAPANESE SENTENCE:

VOCABULARY:

クッキー **kukkī** = cookie

先週 **senshū** = last week

ミルクシェイク **miruku-shēku** = milkshake

忘れます **wasuremasu** = to forget

約束 **yakusoku** = appointment

▪ NOTES ▪

In this section, you are practicing how to say "I am sorry for ... (VERB)." The verb has to be in its て **TE** form: Verb-て **TE** + すみません **sumimasen**.

WRITE THE FOLLOWING IN JAPANESE:

1. I am sorry for eating your cookie (regretfully).

2. I am sorry for forgetting an appointment last week.

3. I am sorry for drinking your milkshake.

1. クッキーを食べてしまってすみません。
2. 先週、約束を忘れてしまってすみません。
3. ミルクシェイクを飲んでしまってすみません。

PHRASE 149

早く　歩きます。

Hayaku　arukimasu.

Quickly　to walk　=　I walk quickly.

COPY THE JAPANESE SENTENCE:

VOCABULARY:

しゃべります **shaberimasu** = to speak

切ります **kirimasu** = to cut

短い **mijikai** = is short

にぎります **nigirimasu** = to hold

うるさい **urusai** = is noisy, is loud

▪ NOTES ▪

In this section, we are learning how to convert い **I** adjectives to adverbs (what modifies verbs). You will need to take off the い **I** and then add く **ku**.

WRITE THE FOLLOWING IN JAPANESE:

1. I cut it short.

2. I am holding on strongly.

3. I am speaking loudly.

1. 短く切りました。
2. 強くにぎります。
3. うるさくしゃべります。

PHRASE 150

元気 に して ください。

Genki ni shite kudasai.

Healthy [PART] to do please = Please be healthy.

COPY THE JAPANESE SENTENCE:

VOCABULARY:

だめ **dame** = is no good

自由 **jiyū** = is free, is liberal

安全 **anzen** = is safe

楽に **raku ni** = easily, comfortably

▪ NOTES ▪

In order to change な **NA** adjectives to the adverbial form, you will need to add に **NI**.

WRITE THE FOLLOWING IN JAPANESE:

1. Please drive safely.

2. Please be free/liberal.

3. Please take it easy.

1. 安全に運転してください。
2. 自由にしてください。
3. 楽にしてください。

PHRASE 151

昨夜 うるさくて、すみません。

Yūbe urusakute, sumimasen.

Last night loud sorry = I am sorry to be loud last night.

COPY THE JAPANESE SENTENCE:

VOCABULARY:

昨夜 **yūbe/sakuya** = last night

今朝 **kesa** = this morning

たまに **tamani** = occasionally

明るい **akarui** = is bright

うるさい **urusai** = is noisy, is loud

▪ NOTES ▪

You can also form the "I am sorry for …" sentence structure with い **I** adjectives, but they must be changed to the adverbial form first as in the example, by dropping い **I** from the adjective and adding くて **KUTE**.

WRITE THE FOLLOWING IN JAPANESE:

1. I am sorry for being late this morning.

2. I am sorry for being loud always.

3. I am sorry that it is (too) bright.

1. 今朝、遅くて、すみません。
2. いつもうるさくて、すみません。
3. 明るくて、すみません。

PHRASE 152

佐藤さん は、運転 しながら、食べて いました。

Satō-san	**wa,**	**unten**	**shinagara,**	**tabete**	**imashita.**
Mr. Sato	[PART]	driving	while	eat	was doing

= Mr. Sato ate while driving.

COPY THE JAPANESE SENTENCE:

VOCABULARY:

ポップコーン **poppukōn** = popcorn

歌います **utaimasu** = to sing

佐藤さん **Satō-san** = Mr./Ms. Sato

コーラ **kōra** = cola

シャワーをあびます **shawā o abimasu** = to take a shower

そうじします **sōji shimasu** = to clean

▪ **NOTES** ▪

In this phrase, the main activity is the first activity, and the secondary activity comes afterwards. The first activity is in the verb stem form and ながら **NAGARA** is added to this verb stem, to indicate that another action is expected after the first action.

WRITE THE FOLLOWING IN JAPANESE:

1. My mom was eating popcorn while watching TV.

2. My dad was singing while taking a shower.

3. I was drinking cola while cleaning.

1. 母は、テレビを見ながら、ポップコーンを食べていました。
2. 父は、シャワーをあびながら、歌っていました。
3. 私は、そうじしながら、コーラを飲んでいました。

PHRASE 153

お好みやき　の　作り方　を、教えていただけませんか。

Okonomiyaki no tsukurikata o oshiete itadakemasen ka.

Japanese savory pancakes [PART] how to make [PART] teach can you do me the favor

= Can you please teach me how to make Japanese savory pancakes?

COPY THE JAPANESE SENTENCE:

VOCABULARY:

いただけませんか **itadakemasen ka**
= can you do me the favor (polite request)

お好みやき **okonomiyaki** = Japanese savory pancakes

消します **keshimasu** = to turn off

調べます **shirabemasu** = to research, to look up

▪ NOTES ▪

いただけませんか **Itadakemasen ka** is a very polite way of asking for a favor. It has the polite form of "to receive" (いただきます **itadakimasu**) and it also has the negative ending, which makes it more indirect and therefore more polite.

WRITE THE FOLLOWING IN JAPANESE:

1. Can you please turn off the lights?

2. Can you please research about Japan?

3. Can you please turn on the TV?

1. 電気を、消していただけませんか。
2. 日本について、調べていただけませんか。
3. テレビを、つけていただけませんか。

PHRASE 154

病気 なら、学校 を 休んで ください。

Byōki nara, gakkō o yasunde kudasai.

Illness if school [PART] to be absent please

= If you are sick, please be absent from school.

COPY THE JAPANESE SENTENCE:

VOCABULARY:

なら **nara** = if

ひま **hima** = free time

大きらい **daikirai** = hate, dislike

ぜひ **zehi** = by all means

ゆうえん地 **yūenchi** = amusement park

▪ NOTES ▪

If you ever travel near Mt. Fuji and love amusement parks, you probably want to stop by Fujikyu Highland. They have many roller coasters that at one time held world records. While on the roller coaster, you will be able to see Mt. Fuji. On this page, we are using the なら **NARA** form with な **NA** adjectives and nouns.

WRITE THE FOLLOWING IN JAPANESE:

1. If you dislike the car, please don't buy it.

2. If you have free time, by all means, please go to the amusement park.

3. If you are healthy, please play soccer.

1. この車がきらいなら、買わないでください。
2. ひまなら、ぜひ、ゆうえん地に行ってください。
3. 元気なら、サッカーをしてください。

PHRASE 155

私　は、べんごし　に　なります。

Watashi wa, bengoshi ni narimasu.

I [PART] lawyer [PART] to become = I will become a lawyer.

COPY THE JAPANESE SENTENCE:

VOCABULARY:

なります **narimasu** = to become

パイロット **pairotto** = pilot

不動産屋 **fudōsanya** = real estate agent

社長 **shachō** = company president

▪ NOTES ▪

On this page なります **narimasu** ("to become") is attached to a NOUN + に **NI** to express one's desire of becoming something (noun). In the next section we will work on adverbs.

WRITE THE FOLLOWING IN JAPANESE:

1. My mom will become a pilot.

2. My dad will become a real estate agent.

3. I will become a company president.

1. 母は、パイロットになります。
2. 父は、不動産屋になります。
3. 私は、社長になります。

PHRASE 156

お水 が 温かく なりました。

O-mizu ga atatakaku narimashita.

Water [PART] warm became = The water has become warm.

COPY THE JAPANESE SENTENCE:

VOCABULARY:

服 **fuku** = clothing

ゆか **yuka** = floor

洗めん所 **senmenjo** = bathroom

娘 **musume** = (my) daughter

▪ NOTES ▪

To show a change in the state of something, the structure い/な **I/NA** ADJECTIVES + く **KU** + なります **narimasu**. For い **I** adjectives, take off the い **I** and add く **ku**. For な **NA** adjectives, just add に **ni.**

WRITE THE FOLLOWING IN JAPANESE:

1. My daughter has become healthy.

2. The bathroom has become dirty.

3. The clothing has become small.

3. 服は、小さくなりました。
2. 洗めん所は、きたなくなりました。
1. 娘は、元気になりました。

PHRASE 157

数学 は、少し むずかしい です。

Sūgaku wa, sukoshi muzukashii desu.

Math [PART] a little difficult [COPULA] = Math is a little difficult.

COPY THE JAPANESE SENTENCE:

VOCABULARY:

数学 **sūgaku** = math

ぶつり **butsuri** = physics

かん字 **kanji** = kanji

けいざい **keizai** = economics

少し **sukoshi** = a little

▪ NOTES ▪

Although you can write any Japanese words using hiragana and katakana, kanji can help you read sentences faster. There are numerous websites and apps that help you read kanji, even the ones you have never seen before.

WRITE THE FOLLOWING IN JAPANESE:

1. Kanji is a little difficult.

____

____

2. Economics is a little difficult.

____

____

3. Physics is a little difficult.

____

____

1. かん字は、少しむずかしいです。
2. けいざいは、少しむずかしいです。
3. ぶつりは、少しむずかしいです。

PHRASE 158

旅行 を した ら、どう ですか。

Ryokō o shita ra, dō desu ka.

Traveling [PART] did if how [COPULA question]

= What if you go on a trip? / How about going on a trip?

COPY THE JAPANESE SENTENCE:

VOCABULARY:

ベランダ **beranda** = balcony

のどあめ **nodoame** = cough drop

なめます **namemasu** = to lick, to suck (a cough drop or candy)

デートします **dēto shimasu** = to date (someone)

▪ NOTES ▪

The たら **TARA** form is the "if" form and the どうですか **dō desu ka** means "How about...?" The どうですか **dō desu ka** ending suggests some action to the listener. Put together, it gives the speaker an opportunity to suggest something.

WRITE THE FOLLOWING IN JAPANESE:

1. What if you date?

____

____

2. What if you have some cough medicine?

____

____

3. What if we eat at the balcony?

____

____

1. デートしたら、どうですか。
2. のどあめをなめたら、どうですか。
3. ベランダで食べたら、どうですか。

PHRASE 159

一度 日本 に 行きたい です

Ichido Nihon ni ikitai desu.

One time Japan [PART] want to go [COPULA]

= I would like to go to Japan once.

COPY THE JAPANESE SENTENCE:

____

____

____

VOCABULARY:

一度 **ichido** = once

二度 **nido** = twice

三度 **sando** = three times

四度 **yondo** = four times

▪ NOTES ▪

度 **DO** means "times" or "frequency." You can attach this to any number to mean the number of times.

WRITE THE FOLLOWING IN JAPANESE:

1. I have been to Japan three times.

2. I would like to eat octopus at least once.

3. I have watched that movie twice.

1. 日本へ三度行ったことがあります。
2. たこを一度食べたいです。
3. その映画を二度見たことがあります。

PHRASE 160

今日、二時間　勉強 しました。

Kyō, ni-jikan benkyō shimashita.

Today, two hours study did = I studied for two hours today.

COPY THE JAPANESE SENTENCE:

VOCABULARY:

間 **kan** = interval of time

じゅ業 **jugyō** = class

プール **pūro** = swimming pool

電車 **densha** = electric train

練習します **renshū shimasu** = to practice

▪ NOTES ▪

Many people spend over one hour commuting to work each way. Some may even spend over two hours one way. Because of the amount of time they are in the train and/or subway, many sleep on it and wake up just in time to get off the train.

WRITE THE FOLLOWING IN JAPANESE:

1. I slept for two hours on the electric train.

2. The class was three hours today.

3. I practiced at the swimming pool for five hours.

1. 電車の中で二時間寝ました。
2. 今日のじゅ業は、三時間でした。
3. プールで五時間練習しました。

PHRASE 161

五日間 休み でした。

Itsuka-kan yasumi deshita.

Five days day off [COPULA IN PAST TENSE] = I had five days off.

COPY THE JAPANESE SENTENCE:

VOCABULARY:

五日間 **itsuka-kan** = for five days

六日間 **muika-kan** = for six days

七日間 **nanoka-kan** = for seven days

八日間 **yōka-kan** = for eight days

▪ NOTES ▪

Pay particular attention to the words for four and eight days since they sound similar. "For four days" is 四日間 **yokka-kan** and "for eight days" is 八日間 **yōka-kan**—they sound almost similar.

WRITE THE FOLLOWING IN JAPANESE:

1. I was in China for eight days.

2. I was in India for seven days.

3. I was sick for six days.

1. 私は、八日間中国にいました。
2. 私は、七日間インドにいました。
3. 私は、六日間病気でした。

PHRASE 162

私　は、九日間　運転　しました。

Watashi wa, kokonoka-kan unten shimashita.

I [PART] nine days drive did = I drove for nine days.

COPY THE JAPANESE SENTENCE:

VOCABULARY:

九日間 **kokonoka-kan** = for nine days

十日間 **tōka-kan** = for ten days

十一日間 **jū-ichi-nichi-kan** = for eleven days

何日間 **nan-nichi-kan** = how many days

▪ NOTES ▪

From the 11th to the end of the month, with the exceptions of 14, 20, and 24, you will just need to add 日 **nichi** to the number to form the number of days.

WRITE THE FOLLOWING IN JAPANESE:

1. I traveled for ten days.

2. I was in the hospital for nine days.

3. How many days did you study?

1. 私は、十日間旅行しました。
2. 私は、十一日間入院しました。
3. 何日間勉強しましたか。

PHRASE 163

私　は、一週間　ギリシャ　に　いました。

Watashi	**wa,**	**isshūkan**	**Girisha**	**ni**	**imashita.**
I	[PART]	one week	Greece	[PART]	was there

= I was in Greece for one week.

COPY THE JAPANESE SENTENCE:

VOCABULARY:

一週間 **isshūkan** = one week

ギリシャ **Girisha** = Greece

二週間 **ni-shūkan** = two weeks

クルーズ **kurūzu** = cruise

▪ NOTES ▪

In order to form the word for a number of weeks, you will need to put the number plus 週間 **shūkan**. The one that is different is 一週間 **isshūkan** (one week).

WRITE THE FOLLOWING IN JAPANESE:

1. I was on a cruise for two weeks.

2. I played tennis for three weeks.

3. I drove for four weeks.

1. 私は、二週間クルーズをしました。
2. 私は、三週間テニスをしました。
3. 私は、四週間運転しました。

PHRASE 164

私　は、一ヶ月　日本　で　勉強　しました。

Watashi wa, ik-kagetsu Nihon de benkyō shimashita.

I [PART] one month Japan [PART] study did

= I studied in Japan for one month.

COPY THE JAPANESE SENTENCE:

VOCABULARY:

二ヶ月 **ni-kagetsu** = two months

四ヶ月 **yon-kagetsu** = four months

十ヶ月 **juk-kagetsu** = ten months

九ヶ月 **kyū-kagetsu** = nine months

▪ NOTES ▪

To give the number of months (as a period of time), the format is a little different from the rest. We use 月 **-getsu** for counting months, e.g. 一ヶ月 **ik-kagetsu** (one month). "Month" as in the name of a month (e.g. January) is 月 **gatsu**: 一月 **ichigatsu**.

WRITE THE FOLLOWING IN JAPANESE:

1. I studied abroad for six months.

2. I traveled for two months.

3. I hiked for one month.

1. 私は、六ヶ月りゅうがくしました。
2. 私は、二ヶ月旅行しました。
3. 私は、一ヶ月ハイキングしました。

PHRASE 165

私　は、二年間　ロサンゼルス　に　住んでいました。

Watashi	**wa,**	**ni-nenkan**	**Rosanzerusu**	**ni**	**sundeimashita.**
I	[PART]	two years	Los Angeles	[PART]	lived

= I lived in Los Angeles for two years.

COPY THE JAPANESE SENTENCE:

VOCABULARY:

二年間 **ni-nenkan** = two years

四年間 **yo-nenkan** = four years

ロサンゼルス **Rosanzerusu** = Los Angeles

オーストラリア **Ōsutoraria** = Australia

▪ **NOTES** ▪

For this phrase, we give the number of years in this format: NUMBER + 年間 **NENKAN.** 年 **Nen** means "years" and 間 **kan** means "interval (time)."

WRITE THE FOLLOWING IN JAPANESE:

1. I lived in Australia for 15 years.

2. I was in college for four years.

3. I lived in Canada for eight years.

1. 私は、十五年間オーストラリアに住んでいました。
2. 私は、四年間大学にいました。
3. 私は、八年間カナダに住んでいました。

PHRASE 166

私　は、一日　に　三度　食べます。

Watashi wa, ichi-nichi ni san-do tabemasu.

I [PART] one day [PART] three times to eat

= I eat three times a day.

COPY THE JAPANESE SENTENCE:

VOCABULARY:

一日に三度 **ichi-nichi ni san-do** = three times a day

ビタミン **bitamin** = vitamin

ラクロス **rakurosu** = lacrosse (game)

野菜ジュース **yasai jūsu** = vegetable juice

▪ NOTES ▪

This phrase is used to express how many times a day you do something. The format is: DAY + に **NI** + NUMBER OF TIMES (..度 **DO**).

WRITE THE FOLLOWING IN JAPANESE:

1. I take vitamins twice a day.

___

___

2. I drink vegetable juice four times a day.

___

___

3. I practice lacrosse once in two days.

___

___

1. 私は、一日に二度ビタミンを飲みます。
2. 私は、一日に四度野菜ジュースを飲みます。
3. 私は、二日間に一度ラクロスを練習します。

PHRASE 167

私　は、ぶた肉　だけ　食べます。

Watashi wa, butaniku dake tabemasu.

I [PART] pork only to eat = I only eat pork.

COPY THE JAPANESE SENTENCE:

VOCABULARY:

だけ **dake** = only

ぶた肉 **butaniku** = pork

クラス **kurasu** = class

音楽 **ongaku** = music

しゅうきょう **shūkyō** = religion

▪ NOTES ▪

Japan's two main religions are Shintoism and Buddhism. Shinto originates from Japan, while Buddhism was started in India. Although a lot of the traditions of these religions are incorporated into everyday life, not as many Japanese people identify themselves as part of an organized religion. Only a small handful of people identify themselves as Christians.

WRITE THE FOLLOWING IN JAPANESE:

1. I only like music class.

2. I only have religion class today.

3. I only drink water.

1. 私は、音楽のクラスだけ好きです。
2. 私は、今日しゅうきょうのクラスだけあります。
3. 私は、水だけ飲みます。

PHRASE 168

私　は、前　日本　に　住んでいました。

Watashi wa, mae Nihon ni sundeimashita.

I [PART] before Japan [PART] lived

= I lived in Japan before.

COPY THE JAPANESE SENTENCE:

VOCABULARY:

選手 **senshu** = athlete

芸能人 **gēnōjin** = celebrity

モンゴル **Mongoru** = Mongolia

前 **mae** = before

▪ NOTES ▪

Similar to the non-specific time words that we have learned previously like "sometimes" and "usually," a particle does not follow the word まえ **mae**. Make sure that at the end of a sentence, you change the verb to its past tense form to match the context.

WRITE THE FOLLOWING IN JAPANESE:

1. I was an athlete before.

2. My dad was a celebrity before.

3. My mom was living in Mongolia before.

1. 私は、前選手でした。
2. 父は、前芸能人でした。
3. 母は、前モンゴルに住んでいました。

PHRASE 169

私 は、今 ポルトガル に 住んでいます。

Watashi wa, ima Porutogaru ni sundeimasu.

I [PART] now Portugal [PART] living

= I live in Portugal now.

COPY THE JAPANESE SENTENCE:

VOCABULARY:

今 **ima** = now

ポルトガル **Porutogaru** = Portugal

キャビンアテンダント **kyabin-atendanto** = flight attendant

コーチ **kōchi** = coach

▪ NOTES ▪

今 **Ima** is similar to 前 **mae** in that it doesn't have a particle after the word. Additionally, since it denotes something that is happening presently, you will need to make sure that the verb is in the regular ます **MASU** form.

WRITE THE FOLLOWING IN JAPANESE:

1. My cousin is a flight attendant now.

____

____

2. My uncle is a coach now.

____

____

3. I am now living in England.

____

____

1. いとこは、今キャビンアテンダントです。
2. おじさんは、今コーチです。
3. 私は、今イギリスに住んでいます。

PHRASE 170

ケンさん　は、りんご　を　二個　食べました。

Ken-san wa, ringo o ni-ko tabemashita.

Ken [PART] apple [PART] two pieces ate

= Ken ate two apples.

COPY THE JAPANESE SENTENCE:

VOCABULARY:

個 **ko** (counter) = counter for small objects

ボール **bōru** = ball

オレンジ **orenji** = orange (fruit)

団子 **dango** = dumpling

▪ NOTES ▪

In Japanese, there are many counters for different types of nouns; 個 **KO** is used for small objects. To count a number of small ones: NUMBER + 個 **KO** (e.g. 二個 **ni-ko** = two small (objects)). Sounds of numbers with 個 **KO** may change: the ones that are special are: 一個 **ik-ko,** 六個 **rok-ko,** and 八個 **hak-ko.**

WRITE THE FOLLOWING IN JAPANESE:

1. I bought three oranges.

2. My mom made seven dumplings.

3. I bought four balls.

1. 私は、オレンジを三個買いました。
2. 母は、団子を七個作りました。
3. 私は、ボールを四個買いました。

PHRASE 171

この 指わ は、 五百 ドル です。

Kono yubiwa wa, go-hyaku doru desu.

This ring [PART] five hundred dollars [COPULA] = This ring costs $500.

COPY THE JAPANESE SENTENCE:

VOCABULARY:

五百 **gohyaku** = 500

三百 **sanbyaku** = 300

六百 **roppyaku** = 600

八百 **happyaku** = 800

▪ NOTES ▪

In this phrase you have learned the word for "hundred." In order to count the hundreds, you will just need to add the number to the word 百 **HYAKU**. Note the sounds for these hundreds: 300, 600, and 800 which are listed above.

WRITE THE FOLLOWING IN JAPANESE:

1. The hat is 850 yen.

____

____

2. Dinner was $250.

____

____

3. The ballpoint pen is 600 yen.

____

____

1. ぼうしは、八百五十円です。
2. 晩ご飯は、二百五十ドルでした。
3. ボールペンは、六百円です。

PHRASE 172

この　車　は、九千　ドル　です。

Kono kuruma wa, kyū-sen doru desu.

This car [PART] 9000 dollars [COPULA] = This car is $9,000.

COPY THE JAPANESE SENTENCE:

VOCABULARY:

千 **sen** = thousand

三千 **sanzen** = 3,000

八千 **hassen** = 8,000

九千 **kyūsen** = 9,000

▪ NOTES ▪

The thousands are quite easy to form as well. Just add 千 **SEN** to the number. The two that have irregular readings for thousands are listed above, which are 3,000 and 8,000. The word for one thousand is just 千 **SEN** (not **ichi-sen**). Please note that the list only goes up to 9,000 and you will learn another word for 10,000 (ten thousand) which will help you form larger numbers.

WRITE THE FOLLOWING IN JAPANESE:

1. The ticket was 9,500 yen.

____

____

2. The chair is 8,300 yen.

____

____

3. The television is 1,300 dollars.

____

____

1. 切符は、九千五百円でした。
2. いすは、八千三百円です。
3. テレビは、千三百ドルです。

PHRASE 173

あの　車　は、　三万　ドル　でした。

Ano　kuruma　wa,　san-man　doru　deshita.

That over there　car　[PART] thirty thousand dollars [COPULA IN PAST TENSE]

= That car over there was $30,000.

COPY THE JAPANESE SENTENCE:

VOCABULARY:

万 **man** = 10,000

十万 **jū-man** = 100,000

百万 **hyaku-man** = one million

七万 **nana-man** = 70,000

▪ NOTES ▪

Learning to think of 10,000 (ten thousand) as 万 **MAN** can be tricky in the beginning, but you will soon get used to it. Always think of how many 10,000 there are to figure out what number it is.

WRITE THE FOLLOWING IN JAPANESE:

1. That ticket is 150,000 yen.

____

____

2. My grandmother's car is 45,000 dollars.

____

____

3. My house is 220,000 dollars.

____

____

1. その切符は、十五万円です。
2. おばあさんの車は、四万五千ドルです。
3. 私のうちは、二十二万ドルです。

PHRASE 174

私　の　家族　は、　五人　です。

Watashi　no　kazoku　wa,　go-nin　desu.

I　[PART]　family　[PART]　five people　[COPULA]

= There are five people in my family.

COPY THE JAPANESE SENTENCE:

VOCABULARY:

五人 **go-nin** = five people

一人 **hitori** = one person

二人 **futari** = two people

三人 **san-nin** = three people

▪ NOTES ▪

The counter 人 **NIN** is used to count people. Except for counting one and two persons, you just need to add 人 **NIN** to the number. You will also need to be careful with four people. The correct form is 四人 **yo-nin**.

WRITE THE FOLLOWING IN JAPANESE:

1. I have three siblings.

____

____

2. There are five hundred students at school.

____

____

3. There are thirty students in the class.

____

____

1. 私の兄弟は、三人です。
2. 学校の生徒は、五百人です。
3. クラスの生徒は、三十人です。

PHRASE 175

紙　を　五枚 ください。

Kami　o　go-mai　kudasai.

Paper [PART] five sheets　give me　= Please give me five sheets of paper.

COPY THE JAPANESE SENTENCE:

VOCABULARY:

枚 **-mai** (counter) = sheet, counter for flat objects

シャツ **shatsu** = shirt

皿 **sara** = plate

ティッシュ **tisshu** = tissue

ナプキン **napukin** = napkin

▪ NOTES ▪

枚 **MAI**, the counter for flat objects, is one of the easiest to remember because there aren't any exceptions for the numbers. To ask how many sheets or flat objects, you would say 何枚 **nan-mai**.

WRITE THE FOLLOWING IN JAPANESE:

1. Please give me four sheets of tissues.

2. There are seven plates on the table.

3. I bought five shirts.

1. ティッシュを四枚ください。
2. テーブルに皿が七枚あります。
3. 私は、シャツを五枚買いました。

PHRASE 176

ガレージ　に　車　が、三台　あります。

Garēji ni kuruma ga, san-dai arimasu.

Garage [PART] car [PART] three there is

= There are three cars in the garage.

COPY THE JAPANESE SENTENCE:

VOCABULARY:

台 **-dai** (counter) = counter for mechanical objects

ガレージ **garēji** = garage

オートバイ **ōtobai** = motorcycle

庭 **niwa** = garden, yard

▪ NOTES ▪

This counter is used for mechanical objects like cars, trains, bikes, and televisions. It is also easy to use as there aren't any changes to the numbers used with this counter.

WRITE THE FOLLOWING IN JAPANESE:

1. There are two motorcycles over there.

2. There are five cars in the yard.

3. There are six bikes at home.

1. あそこにオートバイが、二台あります。
2. 庭に車が、五台あります。
3. うちに自転車が、六台あります。

PHRASE 177

私　は、犬　を　二匹　かっています。

Watashi wa, inu o ni-hiki katteimasu.

I [PART] dog [PART] two to raise = I have two dogs.

COPY THE JAPANESE SENTENCE:

VOCABULARY:

かっています **katteimasu** = to raise (a pet)

匹 **-hiki (-biki/-piki)** (counter) = counter for small animals

一匹 **ip-piki** = one small animal

三匹 **san-biki** = three small animals

六匹 **rop-piki** = six small animals

十匹 **jup-piki** = ten small animals

▪ NOTES ▪

This counter is used only for small animals like dogs, cats, fish, etc. The sound of the counter changes with some numbers: 一匹 **ip-piki** (one), 三匹 **san-biki** (three), 六匹 **rop-piki** (six), 八匹 **hap-piki** (eight), and 十匹 **jup-piki** (ten). With the other numbers, you can just add 匹 **hiki**.

WRITE THE FOLLOWING IN JAPANESE:

1. I have three cats.

2. I have four fish.

3. I have seven pigs.

1. 私は、ねこを三匹かっています。
2. 私は、魚を四匹かっています。
3. 私は、ぶたを七匹かっています。

PHRASE 178

私　は、えんぴつ　を　五本　持っています。

Watashi wa, enpitsu o go-hon motteimasu.

I [PART] pencil [PART] five to have

= I have five pencils.

COPY THE JAPANESE SENTENCE:

VOCABULARY:

本 **-hon (-bon/-pon)** (counter) = counter for long, thin objects

持っています **motteimasu** = holding, have

ストロー **sutorō** = straw

つえ **tsue** = cane

▪ **NOTES** ▪

This counter is used for objects that are long and thin like pencils, canes, bananas, etc. These have different sounds for the counter: 一本 **ip-pon** (one), 三本 **san-bon** (three), 六本 **rop-pon** (six), 八本 **hap-pon** (eight), and 十本 **jup-pon** (ten).

WRITE THE FOLLOWING IN JAPANESE:

1. Please give me five straws.

2. I am holding three canes.

3. Please give me six ballpoint pens.

1. ストローを、五本ください。
2. つえを、三本持っています。
3. ボールペンを、六本ください。

PHRASE 179

私　は、昨日　ビール　を　二杯　飲みました。

Watashi wa, kinō bīru o ni-hai nomimashita.

I [PART] yesterday beer [PART] two cups drank

= I drank two (glasses of) beers yesterday.

COPY THE JAPANESE SENTENCE:

VOCABULARY:

杯 **-hai (-bai/-pai)** (counter) = counter for cupfuls

麦茶 **mugicha** = barley tea

ホテル **hoteru** = hotel

夜中 **yonaka** = middle of the night

▪ NOTES ▪

This counter is used to express the number of cups/mugs used for a drink, etc. The following numerals do not follow the usual counting pattern: 一杯 **ip-pai** (one), 三杯 **san-bai** (three), 六杯 **rop-pai** (six), 八杯 **hap-pai** (eight), and 十杯 **jup-pai** (ten). To ask how many cups, you would say 何杯 **nan-bai**.

WRITE THE FOLLOWING IN JAPANESE:

1. I drank three cups of milk in the middle of the night.

2. I drank two cups of coffee at the hotel.

3. My older sister drank four cups of barley tea.

1. 私は、夜中に牛乳を三杯飲みました。
2. 私は、ホテルでコーヒーを二杯飲みました。
3. 姉は、麦茶を四杯飲みました。

PHRASE 180

私　は、中国　に　三回　行った　こと　が　あります。

Watashi wa, Chūgoku ni san-kai itta koto ga arimasu.

I [PART] China [PART] three times went experience [PART] there is

= I have been to China three times.

COPY THE JAPANESE SENTENCE:

VOCABULARY:

回 **kai** = times (frequency)

げき **geki** = a play

降ります **furimasu** = to rain

泊まります **tomarimasu** = to stay

▪ NOTES ▪

This counter is similar to 度 **DO** that we learned previously. Most of the time, they can be used interchangeably.

WRITE THE FOLLOWING IN JAPANESE:

1. It rained twice today.

____

____

2. I saw this play five times.

____

____

3. I have stayed here three times.

____

____

1. 今日は雨が、二回降りました。
2. このげきを、五回見ました。
3. ここに、三回泊まったことがあります。

PHRASE 181

私　は、アップルパイ　を　二個　も　食べました。

Watashi wa, appuru-pai o ni-ko mo tabemashita.

I [PART] apple pie [PART] two pieces as much as ate

= I ate as many as two apple pies.

COPY THE JAPANESE SENTENCE:

______

______

______

VOCABULARY:

アップルパイ **appuru-pai** = apple pie

も **mo** = as much as, as many as

ウィスキー **wisukī** = whiskey

コンサート **konsāto** = concert

▪ NOTES ▪

You have seen the particle も **MO** in several other sentences to mean "also" and "both." In this phrase, you are learning another meaning of も **MO** "as much as."

WRITE THE FOLLOWING IN JAPANESE:

1. I drank as many as three whiskeys.

____

____

2. There were as many as 20,000 people at the concert.

____

____

3. I went to Japan as many as 20 times.

____

____

3. 私は、日本へ二十回も行きました。
2. コンサートには、二万人もいました。
1. 私は、ウイスキーを三杯も飲みました。

PHRASE 182

私　は、お酒　を　二杯　しか　飲みません　でした。

Watashi wa, o-sake o ni-hai shika nomimasen deshita.

I [PART] alcohol [PART] two cups only not drink [COPULA]

= I only drank two cups of alcohol.

COPY THE JAPANESE SENTENCE:

VOCABULARY:

しか **shika** = (particle) only

発表 **happyō** = presentation

白菜 **hakusai** = Nappa cabbage

お酒 **o-sake** = alcohol, rice wine

▪ NOTES ▪

しか **SHIKA** indicates "no more than," just like the English meaning of "only." The しか **SHIKA** form always needs a negative verb ending.

WRITE THE FOLLOWING IN JAPANESE:

1. I only ate breakfast yesterday.

2. Only three people came to my presentation.

3. My older sister only eats Nappa cabbage.

1. 私は、昨日朝ご飯しか食べませんでした。
2. 私の発表には、三人しか来ませんでした。
3. 姉は、白菜しか食べません。

PHRASE 183

あの　人は、田中さん　だった　よう　です。

Ano hito wa, Tanaka-san datta yō desu.

That over there person [PART] Mr. Tanaka [COPULA] look like [COPULA]

= That person over there looked like Mr. Tanaka.

COPY THE JAPANESE SENTENCE:

VOCABULARY:

昔 **mukashi** = a long time ago

だった **datta** = past tense of **DESU**

教室 **kyōshitsu** = classroom

前 **mae** = before

小屋 **koya** = shed

事務所 **jimusho** = office

▪ NOTES ▪

You can use the ようです **YŌ DESU** form with nouns to express the idea that something or somebody looks like something else. In order to form such sentences, you will need to keep to this structure: NOUN + の **NO** + ようです **yō desu**.

WRITE THE FOLLOWING IN JAPANESE:

1. Here looks like it was a hospital a long time ago.

2. That classroom looks like it was an office previously.

3. This shed looks like it was a house a long time ago.

1. ここは、昔病院だったようです。
2. その教室は、前事務所だったようです。
3. この小屋は、昔うちだったようです。

PHRASE 184

テニス を しよう。

Tenisu o shiyō.

Tennis [PART] let's do = Let's play tennis.

COPY THE JAPANESE SENTENCE:

____

____

____

VOCABULARY:

しよう **shiyō** = let's do

来よう **koyō** = let's come

サッカーをします **sakkā o shimasu** = to play soccer

勉強します **benkyō shimasu** = to study

▪ NOTES ▪

This is the "let's" informal form for Group 3 verbs: します **shimasu** and 来ます **kimasu**. Group 3 verbs do not necessarily follow the usual pattern of verb conjugation, and therefore the "let's" form is listed as above.

WRITE THE FOLLOWING IN JAPANESE:

1. Let's come here again.

2. Let's play soccer.

3. Let's study.

1. またここへ来よう。
2. サッカーをしよう。
3. 勉強しよう。

PHRASE 185

今日　は、　魚　を　食べよう。

Kyō wa, sakana o tabeyō.

Today [PART] fish [PART] let's eat = Let's eat fish today.

COPY THE JAPANESE SENTENCE:

VOCABULARY:

ぶたまん **butaman** = pork buns

ドラマ **dorama** = TV drama

プレゼント **purezento** = present

授業 **jugyō** = class

▪ NOTES ▪

To form the "let's" informal form for Group 2 verbs, you will need to take off the ます **masu** from the verb and add よう **yō**.

WRITE THE FOLLOWING IN JAPANESE:

1. Let's eat pork buns.

2. Let's watch a TV drama.

3. Let's begin class.

1. ぶたまんを食べよう。
2. ドラマを見よう。
3. 授業を始めよう。

PHRASE 186

来週、日本 へ 行こう。

Raishū, Nihon e ikō.

Next week, Japan to let's go = Let's go to Japan next week.

COPY THE JAPANESE SENTENCE:

VOCABULARY:

来週 **raishū** = next week

果物 **kudamono** = fruit

公園 **kōen** = park

海 **umi** = ocean

▪ NOTES ▪

To form the "let's" informal form for Group 1 verbs, you will need to 1) take off the ます **MASU**, 2) change the last character to the /を **o**/ sound of that column on the hiragana chart and 3) add う **u**. For example, if the word is 書きます **kakimasu** the "let's" form will be 書こう **kakō**.

WRITE THE FOLLOWING IN JAPANESE:

1. Let's swim in the ocean.

2. Let's buy some fruit.

3. Let's play at the park.

1. 海で泳ごう。
2. 果物を買おう。
3. 公園で遊ぼう。

PHRASE 187

私　は、テニス　が　出来ます。

Watashi wa, tenisu ga dekimasu.

I [PART] tennis [PART] can do = I can play tennis.

COPY THE JAPANESE SENTENCE:

VOCABULARY:

出来ます **dekimasu** = can do

ギター **gitā** = guitar

バイオリン **baiorin** = violin

サーフィン **sāfin** = surfing

▪ **NOTES** ▪

The が **GA** + 出来ます **DEKIMASU** structure allows you to express what you can do. In order to use this sentence structure, what comes before が **GA** must be a noun, like guitar, surfing, and tennis. 出来ます **Dekimasu** here expresses the ability to do something, and it must always be preceded by が **GA**, not any other particles.

WRITE THE FOLLOWING IN JAPANESE:

1. I can play the guitar.

____

____

2. I can surf.

____

____

3. I can play the violin.

____

____

1. 私は、ギターが出来ます。
2. 私は、サーフィンが出来ます。
3. 私は、バイオリンが出来ます。

PHRASE 188

私　は、日本語　を　話す　こと　が　出来ます。

Watashi wa, Nihon-go o hanasu koto ga dekimasu.

I [PART] Japanese [PART] speak experience [PART] can do

= I can speak Japanese.

COPY THE JAPANESE SENTENCE:

VOCABULARY:

デザート **dezāto** = dessert

打ちます **uchimasu** = to hit

飛びます **tobimasu** = to fly, to jump

日本食 **nihonshoku** = Japanese food

▪ **NOTES** ▪

In the previous phrase, we learned to form the sentence for "I can …" Here, we learn how to say the same thing in another way: VERB-dictionary form + こと **KOTO** and adding が出来ます **ga dekimasu**. Please remember that there are three groups of verbs and you will need to change the verbs accordingly.

WRITE THE FOLLOWING IN JAPANESE:

1. I am able to make dessert.

2. I am able to jump high.

3. I am able to hit a ball.

1. 私は、デザートを作ることが出来ます。
2. 私は、高く飛ぶことが出来ます。
3. 私は、ボールを打つことが出来ます。

PHRASE 189

たくさん 勉強 したら、いい てんすう が とれます。

Takusan benkyō shita ra, ii tensū ga toremasu.

Takusan	**benkyō**	**shita**	**ra,**	**ii**	**tensū**	**ga**	**toremasu.**
A lot	study	to do	if	good	score	[PART]	to take

= If you study a lot, you can get good marks.

COPY THE JAPANESE SENTENCE:

VOCABULARY:

とります **torimasu** = to take

きんトレする **kintore suru** = to train with weights

きん肉 **kinniku** = muscle

なおります **naorimasu** = to become better

▪ **NOTES** ▪

This たら **TARA** structure, for "if" constructions, is formed with VERB (informal past) + ら **RA**. For example, the たら **TARA** form of 飲みます **nomimasu** will be 飲んだら **nonda ra**.

WRITE THE FOLLOWING IN JAPANESE:

1. If you train with weights, your muscles will become bigger.

____

____

2. If you practice, you will become skillful.

____

____

3. If you take medicine, you will become better.

____

____

1. きんトレしたら、きん肉が大きくなります。
2. 練習したら、じょうずになります。
3. 薬を飲んだら、なおります。

PHRASE 190

母　は、明日　日本　へ　行く　はず　です。

Haha wa, ashita Nihon e iku hazu desu.

My mom [PART] tomorrow Japan to to go expected [COPULA]

= My mom is expected to go to Japan tomorrow.

COPY THE JAPANESE SENTENCE:

VOCABULARY:

はず **hazu** = expected

卓球 **takkyū** = ping pong

トランク **toranku** = trunk of a car

冬 **fuyu** = winter

▪ NOTES ▪

The predicative form, as shown above, is created using the informal form of the verb and adding はず **HAZU.**

WRITE THE FOLLOWING IN JAPANESE:

1. This winter is expected to have a lot of snow.

____

____

2. My father is expected to fix my trunk.

____

____

3. My older sister is expected to win in ping pong.

____

____

1. この冬は、たくさん雪が降るはずです。
2. 父は、トランクを直すはずです。
3. 姉は、卓球で勝つはずです。

PHRASE 191

姉　は、母　みたい　に　歩きます。

Ane wa, haha mitai ni arukimasu.

My older sister [PART] my mom similar to [PART] to walk

= My older sister walks like my mom.

COPY THE JAPANESE SENTENCE:

VOCABULARY:

やせています **yaseteimasu** = to be thin

水兵 **suihei** = sailor

床屋 **tokoya** = barber

砂場 **sunaba** = sandbox

▪ **NOTES** ▪

The みたい **MITAI** form is used to express "resembling or similar to something else." It is formed by attaching みたい **mitai** to a noun.

WRITE THE FOLLOWING IN JAPANESE:

1. My mom is thin like a child.

2. My dad is strong like a sailor.

3. School is fun like the sandbox.

1. 母は、子どもみたいにやせています。
2. 父は、水兵みたいに強いです。
3. 学校は、砂場みたいに楽しいです。

PHRASE 192

明日　は、晴れ　だ　と　いい　です。

Ashita wa, hare da to ii desu.

Tomorrow [PART] sunny [COPULA] [PART] good [COPULA]

= It will be great if tomorrow is sunny.

COPY THE JAPANESE SENTENCE:

VOCABULARY:

彼 **kare** = him, he

彼女 **kanojo** = her, she

お金持ち **o-kanemochi** = rich person

茶色 **chairo** = brown

▪ NOTES ▪

The といいです **TO II DESU** form is used to say that it would be good "if ... happens." For this phrase, we focus on nouns and な **NA** adjectives, for which, you will need to add a だ **da** before といいです **to ii desu**.

WRITE THE FOLLOWING IN JAPANESE:

1. It would be great if he is rich.

____

____

2. It would be great if the car is brown.

____

____

3. It would be great if she is skillful in tennis.

____

____

1. 彼は、お金持ちだといいです。
2. 車は、茶色だといいです。
3. 彼女は、テニスがじょうずだといいです。

PHRASE 193

今日　の　晩ご飯　は、おいしい　と　いい　です。

Kyō no ban-gohan wa, oishii to ii desu.

Today [PART] dinner [PART] delicious [PART] good [COPULA]

= It will be great if today's dinner is delicious.

COPY THE JAPANESE SENTENCE:

____

____

____

VOCABULARY:

私たち **watashitachi** = us, we

ぼくたち **bokutachi** = us, we (for boys)

試合 **shiai** = sports game

近い **chikai** = is close, is nearby

▪ **NOTES** ▪

We are now focusing on how to use the といいです **TO II DESU** form with い **I** adjectives. For い **I** adjectives, you just add the といいです **to ii desu** to the い **I** adjective. Note that たち **tachi** is a pluralizing suffix for people.

WRITE THE FOLLOWING IN JAPANESE:

1. It will be great if today's sports game is interesting.

____

____

2. It will be great if school is nearby.

____

____

3. It will be great if our team is strong.

____

____

1. 今日の試合は、おもしろいといいです。
2. 学校は、近いといいです。
3. 私たちのチームは、強いといいです。

PHRASE 194

子ども は、たくさん 食べる と いい です。

Kodomo	**wa,**	**takusan**	**taberu**	**to**	**ii**	**desu.**
Child(ren)	[PART]	a lot	to eat	[PART]	good	[COPULA]

= It will be great if children eat a lot.

COPY THE JAPANESE SENTENCE:

VOCABULARY:

子ども **kodomo** = child(ren)

ニュージーランド **Nyūjīrando** = New Zealand

物 **mono** = things

インフルエンザ **infuruenza** = flu

▪ NOTES ▪

To form the といいです **TO II DESU** form with verbs, they must be in one of the informal forms. You can use them in conjunction with the potential form, as long as you convert the potential form to the informal form. Since all potential forms have /え **e**/ sound before ます **MASU**, every potential verb is in Group 2.

WRITE THE FOLLOWING IN JAPANESE:

1. It will be great if he recovers from the flu.

____

____

2. It will be great if I can eat a lot of delicious things.

____

____

3. It will be great if I can go to New Zealand.

____

____

1. インフルエンザがなおるといいです。
2. たくさんおいしいものが食べられるといいです。
3. ニュージーランドに行けるといいです。

PHRASE 195

日本語　を　教えて　くれて、　ありがとう。

Nihon-go　o　oshiete　kurete,　arigatō.

Japanese　[PART]　teach　give me　thank you

= Thank you for teaching me Japanese.

COPY THE JAPANESE SENTENCE:

VOCABULARY:

運びます **hakobimasu** = to carry

押します **oshimasu** = to push

探します **sagashimasu** = to look for

かぎ **kagi** = keys

▪ NOTES ▪

This phrase combines the て **TE** form along with くれます **KUREMASU** which means "to give to me/my family members." This phrase is used to thank someone for doing you a favor. We will focus here on Group 1 verbs.

WRITE THE FOLLOWING IN JAPANESE:

1. Thank you for carrying the boxes.

2. Thank you for pushing the car.

3. Thank you for looking for my keys.

1. 箱を運んでくれて、ありがとう。
2. 車を押してくれて、ありがとう。
3. かぎを探してくれて、ありがとう。

PHRASE 196

早く　起きて　くれて、ありがとう。

Hayaku okite kurete, arigatō.

Early wake up give me thank you

= Thank you for waking me up early.

COPY THE JAPANESE SENTENCE:

____

____

____

VOCABULARY:

全部 **zenbu** = all, everything

子どもたち **kodomotachi** = children

見せます **misemasu** = to show me

開けます **akemasu** = to open

▪ NOTES ▪

This page focuses on Group 2 verbs and the phrase, "Thank you for VERBing." Remember that the verb needs to be in the て **TE** form which is converted by taking off the ます **MASU** and adding て **TE**.

WRITE THE FOLLOWING IN JAPANESE:

1. Thank you for watching the children.

____

____

2. Thank you for showing me your house.

____

____

3. Thank you for opening the door.

____

____

1. 子どもたちを見てくれて、ありがとう。
2. うちを見せてくれて、ありがとう。
3. ドアを開けてくれて、ありがとう。

PHRASE 197

わざわざ　来て　くれて、ありがとう。

Wazawaza **kite** **kurete,** **arigatō.**

To take the effort to come give me thank you

= Thank you for taking the time to come.

COPY THE JAPANESE SENTENCE:

VOCABULARY:

わざわざ **wazawaza** = taking the time/effort

ゴルフをする **gorufu o suru** = to play golf

ラクロスをする **rakurosu o suru** = to play lacrosse

シートベルトをする **shītoberuto o suru** = to wear a seatbelt

▪ **NOTES** ▪

There are two verbs in Group 3: します **shimasu** and 来ます **kimasu**. However, many verbs are formed using します **shimasu** as given in the Vocabulary list here. These are known as する **SURU** verbs, formed by a NOUN + する **SURU**.

WRITE THE FOLLOWING IN JAPANESE:

1. Thank you for wearing a seatbelt.

____

____

2. Thank you for playing lacrosse with me.

____

____

3. Thank you for playing golf with me.

____

____

1. シートベルトをしてくれて、ありがとう。
2. 一緒にラクロスをしてくれて、ありがとう。
3. 一緒にゴルフをしてくれて、ありがとう。

PHRASE 198

昨日　宿題　を　して、よかった　です。

Kinō　shukudai　o　shite,　yokatta　desu.

Yesterday homework [PART] to do was good [COPULA]

= It was great that I finished my homework yesterday.

COPY THE JAPANESE SENTENCE:

VOCABULARY:

先週 **senshū** = last week

たん生日パーティー **tanjōbi pātī** = birthday party

りゅうがくします **ryūgaku shimasu** = to study abroad

南米 **nanbei** = South America

▪ NOTES ▪

This phrase is used when you want to express thankfulness and/or exhilaration for doing something. We are focusing on Group 3 verbs on this page.

WRITE THE FOLLOWING IN JAPANESE:

1. It was great that I studied abroad in South America.

2. It was great that you came to my house last week.

3. It was great that you came to my mom's birthday party.

1. 南米へりゅうがくして、よかったです。
2. 先週私の家へ来てくれて、よかったです。
3. 母のたん生日パーティーに来てくれてよかったです。

PHRASE 199

たくさん　おいしい　物　を 食べられて、よかった です。

Takusan	**oishii**	**mono**	**o**	**taberarete,**	**yokatta**	**desu**
A lot	delicious	things	[PART]	can eat	was good	[COPULA]

= It was great that I could eat a lot of delicious things.

COPY THE JAPANESE SENTENCE:

VOCABULARY:

うに **uni** = sea urchin

イタリア **Itaria** = Italy

うなぎ **unagi** = eel

いくら **ikura** = salmon roe

▪ NOTES ▪

Sea urchin and salmon roe are some of the most expensive sushi. Some people like them a lot, while others don't like them at all. The texture for each might turn some people off.

WRITE THE FOLLOWING IN JAPANESE:

1. It was great that I was able to eat eel.

2. It was great that I was able to watch an Italian movie.

3. It was great that I was able to eat sea urchin.

1. うなぎが食べられて、よかったです。
2. イタリアの映画が見られて、よかったです。
3. うにが食べられて、よかったです。

PHRASE 200

日本 へ 行けて、よかった です。

Nihon e ikete, yokatta desu.

Japan to able to go was good [COPULA]

= It was great that I was able to go to Japan.

COPY THE JAPANESE SENTENCE:

VOCABULARY:

家具 **kagu** = furniture

コロンビア **Koronbia** = Columbia

桃 **momo** = peach

コーラ **kōra** = Cola

▪ NOTES ▪

In Japan, you will be able to taste fruit that is absolutely delicious. You can buy special fruit that are very expensive but taste very sweet and out of this world from supermarts located in the basement of department stores. Peach and melon are some of the fruit that you might want to sample.

WRITE THE FOLLOWING IN JAPANESE:

1. It was great that I was able to drink peach juice.

2. It was great that I was able to buy furniture.

3. It was great that I was able to go to Columbia.

1. 桃のジュースが飲めて、よかったです。
2. 家具が買えて、よかったです。
3. コロンビアへ行けて、よかったです。

PHRASE 201

日本　へ　行く　と、いつも　時差ぼけ　が　大変　です。

Nihon e iku to, itsumo jisa-boke ga taihen desu.

Japan to to go when always jetlag [PART] difficult [COPULA]

= Whenever I go to Japan, the jetlag is dreadful.

COPY THE JAPANESE SENTENCE:

____

____

____

VOCABULARY:

と、いつも **to itsumo** = whenever

時差ぼけ **jisa-boke** = jetlag

大変 **taihen** = is difficult, is dreadful

具合が悪い **guai ga warui** = not feeling good

夜 **yoru** = night

▪ NOTES ▪

In this phrase, と **TO** means "if" or "when." The dictionary form of the verb needs to precede the と **TO**. On this page, we will focus on Group 1 verbs.

WRITE THE FOLLOWING IN JAPANESE:

1. Whenever I drink alcohol, I don't feel well.

2. Whenever I read a book at night, I feel sleepy.

3. Whenever I go to Japan, I eat a lot of ramen.

1. お酒を飲むと、いつも具合が悪くなります。
2. 夜、本を読むと、いつも眠くなります。
3. 日本へ行くと、いつもラーメンを食べます。

PHRASE 202

ホラー映画　を　見る　と、こわく　なります。

Horā eiga　o　miru　to,　kowaku　narimasu.

Horror movie [PART] watch when scared to become

= When I watch a horror movie, I get scared. (I will be scared.)

COPY THE JAPANESE SENTENCE:

VOCABULARY:

ホラー映画 **horā eiga** = horror movie

体 **karada** = body

こわくなります **kowaku narimasu** = to be scared

元気 **genki** = is energetic

温かい **atatakai** = is warm

▪ **NOTES** ▪

Japan produces many horror movies that have become very popular in other countries including *The Ring* and *The Revenge*. On this page, we are focusing on Group 2 verbs using と **to** phrases.

WRITE THE FOLLOWING IN JAPANESE:

1. When I run, my body warms up.

2. When I eat Korean barbeque, I become happy.

3. When I sing, I become energetic.

1. 走ると、体が温かくなります。
2. やき肉を食べると、うれしくなります。
3. 歌うと、元気になります。

PHRASE 203

テニス を する と、汗 を かきます。

Tenisu o suru to, ase o kakimasu.

Tennis [PART] to do when sweat [PART] to sweat

= When I play tennis, I sweat.

COPY THE JAPANESE SENTENCE:

VOCABULARY:

汗をかきます **ase o kakimasu** = to sweat

ドキドキします **dokidoki shimasu** = to be nervous

けんかします **kenka shimasu** = to fight, to quarrel

悲しい **kanashii** = is sad

▪ NOTES ▪

In Japan, when a person passes away, he/she is cremated. There is usually a family plot where the ashes are brought to.

WRITE THE FOLLOWING IN JAPANESE:

1. When I get nervous, I sweat.

2. When my family comes, I become happy.

3. When I fight with my friend, I become sad.

1. ドキドキすると、汗をかきます。
2. 家族が来ると、うれしくなります。
3. 友だちとけんかすると、悲しくなります。

PHRASE 204

品物　を　さわらない　で　ください。

Shinamono o sawaranai de kudasai.

Merchandise [PART] not touch [PART] please

= Please do not touch the merchandise.

COPY THE JAPANESE SENTENCE:

___

___

___

VOCABULARY:

さわります **sawarimasu** = to touch

品物 **shinamono** = merchandise

汚い **kitanai** = is dirty

写真をとります **shashin o torimasu** = to take a picture

▪ NOTES ▪

This form uses the ない **NAI** form, which is the informal negative form, and attaching it to でください **DE KUDASAI** the statement becomes a request NOT to do something. If you leave out the ください **kudasai**, it can be a command not to do something.

WRITE THE FOLLOWING IN JAPANESE:

1. Don't cry.

2. Please don't take pictures.

3. Don't buy it.

1. 泣かないで。
2. 写真をとらないでください。
3. 買わないで。

PHRASE 205

予約　しない　で　　ね。

Yoyaku　shinai　de　ne.

Reservation　do not　[PART] [CONFIRMATION]　=　Don't make a reservation, ok?

COPY THE JAPANESE SENTENCE:

VOCABULARY:

予約します **yoyaku shimasu** = to make a reservation

心配します **shinpai shimasu** = to worry

アクセサリーをつけます **akusesarī o tsukemasu** = to wear accessories

そうじします **sōji shimasu** = to clean

▪ NOTES ▪

心配しないで **Shinpai shinai de** is a useful phrase to know. You can use this as a reply after someone thanks you for a favor you are doing for them or apologizes after making a mistake. It means "Not to worry."

WRITE THE FOLLOWING IN JAPANESE:

1. Please don't worry, ok?

2. Please don't do cleaning today, ok?

3. Please don't wear accessories, ok?

1. 心配しないでくださいね。
2. 今日は、そうじしないでくださいね。
3. アクセサリーをつけないでくださいね。

PHRASE 206

私　は、　生物学　を　勉強　して　も、　わかりません。

Watashi wa, seibutsugaku o benkyō shite mo, wakarimasen.

I [PART] biology [PART] study to do even though not understand

= Even though I studied biology, I don't understand.

COPY THE JAPANESE SENTENCE:

VOCABULARY:

歩いて来ます **aruite-kimasu** = to come on foot

おこっています **okotteimasu** = to be mad/angry

愛します **aishimasu** = to be in love

自己紹介します **jikoshōkai shimasu** = to do a self-introduction

▪ NOTES ▪

The ても **TE MO** form is used when you want to express "although." In order to form phrases of this nature, you will need to convert the verb to the て **TE** form and then add も **MO**. On this page, we will concentrate on Group 3 verbs.

WRITE THE FOLLOWING IN JAPANESE:

1. Even though I did my self-introduction, my friends forgot my name.

2. Although I came on foot, there wasn't any school.

3. Although I love you, I am mad.

1. 自己紹介しても、友だちは私の名前を忘れました。
2. 歩いて来ても、学校はありませんでした。
3. あなたを愛していても、私はおこっています。

PHRASE 207

母　は、たくさん　食べて　も、　太りません。

Haha　wa,　takusan　tabete　mo,　futorimasen.

My mom [PART]　a lot　eat　even though,　not be fat

= Even though she eats a lot, my mom doesn't get fat.

COPY THE JAPANESE SENTENCE:

VOCABULARY:

太ります **futorimasu** = to get fat

意味 **imi** = meaning

文しょう **bunsho** = sentence

へります **herimasu** = to decrease

答えます **kotaemasu** = to answer

▪ NOTES ▪

This page focuses on Group 2 verbs using the ても **TE MO** form.

WRITE THE FOLLOWING IN JAPANESE:

1. Even though I read the sentence four times, I didn't understand its meaning.

___

___

2. Even though I answered the question, it was wrong.

___

___

3. Even though I ate a lot, the amount of cake wasn't depleted.

___

___

1. 文しょうを四回読んでも、意味がわかりませんでした。
2. 質問に答えても、間違えました。
3. たくさん食べても、ケーキがへりません。

PHRASE 208

たくさん 水 を 飲んで も、 まだ のど が かわいています。

Takusan mizu o nonde mo, mada nodo ga kawaiteimasu.

A lot water [PART] drink even though, still throat [PART] to be dry

= Even though I drank a lot of water, I am still thirsty.

COPY THE JAPANESE SENTENCE:

VOCABULARY:

のどがかわいています **nodo ga kawaiteimasu** = is thirsty

やせます **yasemasu** = to lose weight

つかれています **tsukareteimasu** = to be tired

負けます **makemasu** = to lose (a game, match, etc.), to be defeated

▪ NOTES ▪

This page focuses on Group 1 verbs using the ても **TE MO** form. Remember that the majority of verbs are Group 1 verbs.

WRITE THE FOLLOWING IN JAPANESE:

1. Even though I run every day, I don't lose weight at all.

2. Even though I sleep a lot, I am still tired.

3. Even though I practiced a lot, I still lost.

1. 私は、毎日走っても、全然やせません。
2. たくさん寝ても、まだつかれています。
3. たくさん練習しても、負けました。

PHRASE 209

私 は、今朝 何も 食べません でした。

Watashi wa, kesa nani mo tabemasen deshita.

I [PART] this morning anything not eat [COPULA PAST]

= I didn't eat anything this morning.

COPY THE JAPANESE SENTENCE:

VOCABULARY:

旅行中 **ryokōchū** = during the trip

クリスマス **kurisumasu** = Christmas

今朝 **kesa** = this morning

あげます **agemasu** = to give

何も **nani mo** = anything, nothing

▪ NOTES ▪

なにも **NANI MO** means "nothing" or "anything." The end of the sentence must be in the negative form of the verb. Therefore, instead of like 食べます **tabemasu**, it must be 食べません **tabemasen**.

WRITE THE FOLLOWING IN JAPANESE:

1. I did not give anything for Christmas.

2. I did not drink anything this morning.

3. I did not buy anything during the trip.

1. クリスマスに、何もあげませんでした。
2. 今朝、何も飲みませんでした。
3. 旅行中に、何も買いませんでした。

PHRASE 210

冬休み に、どこへも 行きません でした。

Fuyu-yasumi	**ni**	**doko e mo**	**ikimasen**	**deshita.**
Winter break	[PART]	nowhere	not go	[COPULA PAST]

= I didn't go anywhere during winter break.

COPY THE JAPANESE SENTENCE:

VOCABULARY:

どこへも **doko e mo** = nowhere

冬休み **fuyu-yasumi** = winter break

週末 **shūmatsu** = weekend

平日 **heijitsu** = weekday

▪ **NOTES** ▪

You can use the どこへも **DOKO E MO** phrase in a sentence to express "nowhere" or "anywhere." Similar to the previous phrases, this phrase needs a negative verb ending.

WRITE THE FOLLOWING IN JAPANESE:

1. I did not go anywhere during the weekend.

2. I did not go anywhere during the weekday.

3. I didn't go anywhere yesterday.

1. 週末に、どこへも行きませんでした。
2. 平日に、どこへも行きませんでした。
3. 昨日、どこへも行きませんでした。

PHRASE 211

おいしい　の　なら、食べたい　です。

Oishii **no** **nara,** **tabetai** **desu.**

Delicious [PART] if want to eat [COPULA]

= I want to eat it if it is delicious.

COPY THE JAPANESE SENTENCE:

VOCABULARY:

明るい **akarui** = is bright

寒い **samui** = is cold

エアコン **eakon** = air conditioner

あつい **atsui** = is hot

▪ NOTES ▪

Please note that on the sample phrase, we added a の **NO** after おいしい **oishii** to express "the one." For い **I** adjectives, you can directly attach なら **NARA** to the adjective.

WRITE THE FOLLOWING IN JAPANESE:

1. If it is cold, wear a jacket.

2. If it is hot, turn on the air conditioner.

3. If it is bright, wear sunglasses.

1. 寒いなら、ジャケットを着てください。
2. あついなら、エアコンをつけてください。
3. 明るいなら、サングラスをかけてください。

PHRASE 212

日本 へ 行く なら、京都 を かん光 して ください。

Nihon	**e**	**iku**	**nara,**	**Kyōto**	**o**	**kankō**	**shite**	**kudasai.**
Japan	to	to go	if	Kyoto	[PART]	tour	to do	please

= If you go to Japan, please tour Kyoto.

COPY THE JAPANESE SENTENCE:

VOCABULARY:

京都 **Kyōto** = Kyoto (city)

青森 **Aomori** = Aomori (pref.)

かん光します **kankō shimasu** = to tour

本物 **honmono** = the real thing

りんご **ringo** = apple

高級な **kōkyū na** = well made, high class

▪ NOTES ▪

To use the なら **NARA** form with verbs, the verb must be in the dictionary form. On this page, we will focus on Group 1 verbs.

WRITE THE FOLLOWING IN JAPANESE:

1. If you are going to Aomori, please eat apples.

____

____

2. If you are buying a car, buy an expensive one.

____

____

3. If you are going to Italy, eat real pizza.

____

____

1. 青森へ行くなら、りんごを食べてください。
2. 車を買うなら、高級なのを買ってください。
3. イタリアへ行くなら、本物のピザを食べてください。

PHRASE 213

ハンバーガー を 食べるなら、チーズバーガー を 食べましょう。

Hanbāgā	o	taberu	nara,	chīzubāgā	o	tabemashō.
Hamburger	[PART]	to eat	if	cheese burger	[PART]	let's eat

= If we are going to eat a hamburger, let's eat a cheese burger.

COPY THE JAPANESE SENTENCE:

VOCABULARY:

中華料理 **chūkaryōri** = Chinese food

やきそば **yakisoba** = fried noodles

スポーツ **spōtsu** = sport, exercise

語学 **gogaku** = language

始めます **hajimemasu** = to start

習います **naraimasu** = to learn

▪ NOTES ▪

All types of food are available in Japan. You are able to find food from around the world, especially in major cities in Japan.

WRITE THE FOLLOWING IN JAPANESE:

1. If we are eating Chinese food, let's eat fried noodles.

____

____

2. If we are going to start exercises, let's start tennis.

____

____

3. If we are going to learn a language, let's study Japanese.

____

____

1. 中華料理を食べるなら、やきそばを食べましょう。
2. スポーツを始めるなら、テニスを始めましょう。
3. 語学を習うなら、日本語を勉強しましょう。

PHRASE 214

うち に 来る なら、明日 来て ください。

Uchi ni kuru nara, ashita kite kudasai.

House [PART] come if, tomorrow come please

= If you are coming to my house, please come tomorrow.

COPY THE JAPANESE SENTENCE:

VOCABULARY:

エジプト **Ejiputo** = Egypt

モロッコ **Morokko** = Morocco

フロリダ **Furorida** = Florida

かん光地 **kankōchi** = tourist spots

▪ NOTES ▪

This page focuses on using the なら **NARA** form with Group 3 verbs.

WRITE THE FOLLOWING IN JAPANESE:

1. If you are coming to Morocco, please come next week.

2. If you are coming to Egypt, let's go see the tourist spots.

3. If you want to play tennis, let's go to the park.

1. モロッコに来るなら、来週来てください。
2. エジプトに来るなら、かん光地を見ましょう。
3. テニスをしたいなら、公園へ行きましょう。

PHRASE 215

私　は、午前中　なら、いつでも　空いています。

Watashi wa, gozenchū nara, itsudemo aiteimasu.

I [PART] in the morning if anytime free

= I am free anytime in the morning.

COPY THE JAPANESE SENTENCE:

VOCABULARY:

午前中 **gozenchū** = in the morning

空いています **aiteimasu** = available, free

以降 **ikō** = after, since, thereafter

来週 **raishū** = next week

▪ NOTES ▪

いつでも **ITSUDEMO** is used to express "anytime." This form is easy to use since it does not involve any negative verb forms.

WRITE THE FOLLOWING IN JAPANESE:

1. Please come to my house anytime after 5:00.

2. I am available anytime next week.

3. I am able to go to Japan anytime next month.

3. 来月なら、いつでも日本へ行けます。
2. 来週なら、いつでも空いています。
1. 五時以降なら、いつでもうちに来てください。

PHRASE 216

私　は、毎日　練習　した　のに、負けました。

Watashi wa, mainichi renshū shita no ni, makemashita.

I [PART] every day practice did but lost

= I practice every day, but I still lost.

COPY THE JAPANESE SENTENCE:

VOCABULARY:

のに **no ni** = despite, but

くやしい **kuyashī** = is regretful, is sad

点数 **tensū** = score

悪い **warui** = is bad

ふらふら **furafura** = is dizzy

▪ **NOTES** ▪

The のに **NO NI** form shows that despite the first action being done, something else happened. It can be translated as "but," "however," or "despite/in spite of." Usually what comes before is in the informal form.

WRITE THE FOLLOWING IN JAPANESE:

1. I drank a lot of water, but I am still dizzy.

2. I studied a lot, but I still had a bad score.

3. Despite winning, I am (still) sad.

1. 私は、たくさん水を飲んだのに、ふらふらです。
2. 私は、たくさん勉強したのに、点数が悪かった。
3. 私は、勝ったのに、くやしい。

PHRASE 217

私　の　友だち　は、「映画 は よかった」と、言いました。

Watashi no tomodachi wa, "eiga wa yokatta" to, iimashita.

I [PART] friend [PART] movie [PART] was good [PART] said

= My friend said, "The movie was good."

COPY THE JAPANESE SENTENCE:

VOCABULARY:

言います **iimasu** = to say

つまらない **tsumaranai** = is boring

気持ち悪い **kimochi-warui** = is disgusting

かしこい **kashikoi** = is smart

におい **nioi** = odor

▪ NOTES ▪

To quote someone in Japanese, you will say PERSON は **WA** THE SENTENCE と、いいます **TO, IIMASU**. It is easy to form because you can just put the sentence the person said in quotes (「 」) after は **wa**.

WRITE THE FOLLOWING IN JAPANESE:

1. My older sister said that the class was boring.

2. My mom said that my younger brother is smart.

3. My older brother said the odor was disgusting.

1. 姉は、「じゅ業はつまらない」と、言いました。
2. 母は、「弟はかしこい」と、言いました。
3. 兄は、「においが気持ち悪い」と、言いました。

PHRASE 218

晩ご飯　を 食べている 間　に、電話　が かかってきました。

Ban-gohan　o　tabeteiru　aida　ni,　denwa　ga　kakatte-kimashita.

Dinner [PART] eating while [PART] phone [PART] had a call

= While I was eating dinner, the phone rang.

COPY THE JAPANESE SENTENCE:

VOCABULARY:

間 **aida** = while

います **imasu** = to stay

ている間に **teiru aida ni** = while I was ... [VERBing]

電話がかかってきます **denwa ga kakatte-kimasu**
= (the phone) rang

▪ NOTES ▪

This phrase is used when you like to express that while you were doing something, another event occurred. The first verb must be in the て **TE** form.

WRITE THE FOLLOWING IN JAPANESE:

1. While I was doing homework, I fell asleep (regretfully).

2. While I was eating, my friend came.

3. While I was about to go to Japan, I had tests.

1. 宿題をしている間に、寝てしまいました。
2. 私が食べている間に、友だちが来ました。
3. 日本に行っている間に、しけんがありました。

PHRASE 219

私　は、友だち　に　笑われました。

Watashi wa, tomodachi ni warawaremashita.

I [PART] friend [PART] be laughed at

= I was laughed at by my friend.

COPY THE JAPANESE SENTENCE:

VOCABULARY:

笑います **waraimasu** = to laugh

どろぼう **dorobō** = robber

盗みます **nusumimasu** = to steal

迷惑をかけます **meiwaku o kakemasu** = to be inconvenienced

▪ NOTES ▪

The passive form is used when you want to express your dissatisfaction for something that someone has done to you. On this page, we will focus on Group 1 verbs: you will need to 1) take off the ます **MASU**, 2) change the last character to the /**a**/ sound in the column of the hiragana chart and 3) add れます **REMASU**. For example, for 買います **kaimasu**, it would be 買われます **kawaremasu.**

WRITE THE FOLLOWING IN JAPANESE:

1. My wallet was stolen by a robber.

2. My pencil was taken by my younger brother.

3. I was inconvenienced by my friend.

1. 私は、どろぼうにさいふを盗まれました。
2. 私は、弟にえんぴつを取られました。
3. 私は、友だちに迷惑をかけられました。

PHRASE 220

友だち　に、私　の　ピザ　を　食べられました。

Tomodachi	**ni**	**watashi**	**no**	**piza**	**o**	**taberaremashita.**
My friend	[PART]	I	[PART]	pizza	[PART]	was eaten

= My pizza was eaten by my friend.

COPY THE JAPANESE SENTENCE:

___

___

___

VOCABULARY:

ビデオ **bideo** = video

ステーキ **sutēki** = steak

いちご **ichigo** = strawberry

ピザ **piza** = pizza

▪ NOTES ▪

To form the passive form of Group 2 verbs, you will need to 1) take off the ます **MASU** and 2) add られます **RAREMASU**. For example, for みます **mimasu**, it would be みられます **miraremasu**. られます **raremasu** verbs are used to show the inconvenience or annoyance caused by someone's action.

WRITE THE FOLLOWING IN JAPANESE:

1. My video was seen by my friend.

____

____

2. My steak was eaten by my dad.

____

____

3. My strawberries were eaten by my dog.

____

____

1. 私は、友だちにビデオを見られました。
2. 父に、私のステーキを食べられました。
3. 犬に、私のいちごを食べられました。

PHRASE 221

私　は、同級生　に　紹介されました。

Watashi wa, dōkyūsei ni shōkai saremashita.

I [PART] the classmate [PART] was introduced

= I was introduced to someone by a classmate.

COPY THE JAPANESE SENTENCE:

VOCABULARY:

されます **saremasu** = passive form of します **shimasu**

来られます **koraremasu** = passive form of 来ます **kimasu**

紹介します **shōkai shimasu** = to introduce

同級生 **dōkyūsei** = classmate

好かれます **sukaremasu** = to like

そんけいします **sonkei shimasu** = to respect

▪ NOTES ▪

As always, Group 3 verbs are a special group of verbs. As noted above, the passive form of します **shimasu** is されます **saremasu** and the passive form of 来ます **kimasu** is 来られます **koraremasu**.

WRITE THE FOLLOWING IN JAPANESE:

1. I was made to drink alcohol by my friend.

2. My dad is liked by the children.

3. The teacher is respected by the students.

1. 私は、友だちにお酒を飲まされました。
2. 父は、子どもたちに好かれています
3. 先生は、生徒にそんけいされています。

PHRASE 222

窓　は、閉めて　あります。

Mado　wa,　shimete　arimasu.

Window [PART]　close　have been done　=　The window has been closed.

COPY THE JAPANESE SENTENCE:

VOCABULARY:

(て)あります **(te) arimasu** = have been done (on purpose)

閉めます **shimemasu** = to close

開けます **akemasu** = to open

かけます **kakemasu** = to pour over

▪ NOTES ▪

The てあります **TE ARIMASU** form is used to express something that someone has done on purpose. The person who has done it is not named in these sentences.

WRITE THE FOLLOWING IN JAPANESE:

1. The door has been closed.

2. The sauce has been poured/drizzled.

3. The window has been opened.

1. ドアは、閉めてあります。
2. ソースは、かけてあります。
3. 窓は、開けてあります。

PHRASE 223

米　　は、買って　あります。

Kome **wa,** **katte** **arimasu.**

Uncooked rice [PART] to buy have been done

= Uncooked rice has been bought.

COPY THE JAPANESE SENTENCE:

VOCABULARY:

米 **kome** = uncooked rice

置きます **okimasu** = to put on, to leave

直します **naoshimasu** = to fix

▪ NOTES ▪

This page focuses on the てあります **TE ARIMASU** form using Group 1 verbs.

WRITE THE FOLLOWING IN JAPANESE:

1. The car has been fixed.

2. The money has been left on the table.

3. The vegetables have been bought.

1. 車は、直してあります。
2. お金は、置いてあります。
3. 野菜は、買ってあります。

PHRASE 224

予約　して　あります。

Yoyaku　shite　arimasu.

Reservation to do have been done = The reservations have been made.

COPY THE JAPANESE SENTENCE:

VOCABULARY:

予約します **yoyaku shimasu** = to make a reservation

電話します **denwa shimasu** = to phone

タイプします **taipu shimasu** = to type

放送します **hōsō shimasu** = to broadcast

▪ NOTES ▪

The てあります **TE ARIMASU** form is used on this page with Group 3 verbs. Not all verbs make sense with the てあります **TE ARIMASU** form so it would be good to double-check to make sure.

WRITE THE FOLLOWING IN JAPANESE:

1. The report has been typed.

2. The phone call has been made.

3. It has been broadcast.

1. タイプしてあります。
2. 電話してあります。
3. 放送してあります。

PHRASE 225

コンピューター　で、　写真　を　大きく　します。

Konpyūtā	**de**	**shashin**	**o**	**ōkiku**	**shimasu.**
Computer	[PART]	photo	[PART]	big	to do

= I will make the picture bigger on the computer.

COPY THE JAPANESE SENTENCE:

VOCABULARY:

大きい **ōkii** = is big

小さい **chisai** = is small

洗たく機 **sentakuki** = washer

汚い **kitanai** = is dirty

軽い **karui** = is light (weight)

▪ NOTES ▪

In this phrase, we add く **KU** + します **SHIMASU** to change an adjective into an adverbial phrase. This means to make something more ADVERB. For い **I** adjectives, you will need to first convert it to the adverb form by taking off the い **I** and adding く **ku** and します **shimasu**. For example, "to make something bad" would be 悪くします **warukushimasu**.

WRITE THE FOLLOWING IN JAPANESE:

1. Don't make the clothes shrink (i.e. make smaller) by the washer.

2. Don't dirty your room.

3. Please lighten this bag.

1. 洗たく機で、服を小さくしないでください。
2. 部屋を汚くしないでください。
3. この袋を軽くしてください。

PHRASE 226

テーブル を きれい に します。

Tēburu	**o**	**kirei**	**ni**	**shimasu.**	
Table	[PART]	clean	[PART]	to do	= I will clean up the table.

COPY THE JAPANESE SENTENCE:

VOCABULARY:

きれい **kirei** = is clean, is pretty

有名 **yūmei** = is famous

大事 **daiji** = is important

安全 **anzen** = is safe

静か **shizuka** = is quiet

▪ **NOTES** ▪

On this page we want to use く **KU** + します **SHIMASU** with な **NA** adjectives: first convert the な **NA** adjective to the adverb form by adding に **ni** and then adding します **shimasu**. For example, "to make safe" would be 安全にします **anzen ni shimasu**.

WRITE THE FOLLOWING IN JAPANESE:

1. I will make you famous.

2. I will make the class quiet.

3. We will make the park safe.

1. 私は、あなたを有名にします。
2. 私は、クラスを静かにします。
3. 私たちは、公園を安全にします。

PHRASE 227

来週、　ゆうえん地　に　行く　こと　に　しました。

Raishū, yūenchi ni iku koto ni shimashita.

Next week amusement park [PART] to go experience [PART] did

= I have decided to go to the amusement park next week.

COPY THE JAPANESE SENTENCE:

VOCABULARY:

バドミントン **badominton** = badminton

物理 **butsuri** = physics

プロテイン **purotein** = protein

ゆうえん地 **yūenchi** = amusement park

▪ **NOTES** ▪

In this phrase, we take the dictionary form, nominalize it by adding こと **KOTO** and します **SHIMASU** to come up with the phrase, "I have decided on VERBing"

WRITE THE FOLLOWING IN JAPANESE:

1. My mom decided to practice badminton every day.

2. My dad decided to drink protein every day.

3. My older sister decided to study physics tomorrow.

1. 母は、毎日バドミントンを練習することにしました。
2. 父は、毎日プロテインを飲むことにしました。
3. 姉は、明日物理を勉強することにしました。

PHRASE 228

私　は、母　に　そうじ　を、手伝わ　されました。

Watashi wa, haha ni sōji o, tetsudawa saremashita.

I [PART] my mom [PART] cleaning [PART] help was forced to do

= I was forced to help in the cleaning by my mom.

COPY THE JAPANESE SENTENCE:

VOCABULARY:

手伝います **tetsudaimasu** = to help

歌います **utaimasu** = to sing

貸します **kashimasu** = to lend

呼びます **yobimasu** = to call

▪ NOTES ▪

To convert verbs to the causative-passive form, first take off the ます **MASU**, change the last character to the /あ **a**/ sound of the column on the hiragana chart and add されます **SAREMASU.** If the last character in step two is し **SHI**, change the last character to the /あ **a**/ sound of the column on the hiragana chart, but you will add せられます **seraremasu**.

WRITE THE FOLLOWING IN JAPANESE:

1. My dad was made to sing by my mom.

____

____

2. I was forced to buy a pencil by my friend.

____

____

3. My younger brother was forced to drink coffee by my older sister.

____

____

1. 父は、母に歌わされました。
2. 私は、友だちにえんぴつを、買わされました。
3. 弟は、姉にコーヒーを、飲まされました。

PHRASE 229

私　は、友だち　に　いくら　を、食べ　させられました。

Watashi wa, tomodachi ni ikura o, tabe saseraremashita.

I [PART] friend [PART] salmon roe [PART] eat was forced to

= I was forced to eat salmon roe by my friend.

COPY THE JAPANESE SENTENCE:

___

___

___

VOCABULARY:

ホラー映画 **horā eiga** = horror movies

いくら **ikura** = salmon roe

起こします **okoshimasu** = to wake up

閉めます **shimemasu** = to close

▪ NOTES ▪

This phrase uses the causative-passive form with Group 2 verbs. All you have to do is take off the ます **MASU** and add させられます **SASERAREMASU**. For example, the causative-passive form of 食べます **tabemasu** is 食べさせられます **tabesaseraremasu**.

WRITE THE FOLLOWING IN JAPANESE:

1. My mom was forced to watch horror movies.

2. My dad was forced to close the window.

3. My older brother was forced to wake up early.

1. 母は、ホラー映画を見させられました。
2. 父は、窓を閉めさせられました。
3. 兄は、早く起こされました。

PHRASE 230

私　は、　母　　に　洗たく　を　させられました。

Watashi wa, haha ni sentaku o saseraremashita.

I [PART] my mom [PART] laundry [PART] was forced to do

= I was forced to do the laundry by my mom.

COPY THE JAPANESE SENTENCE:

VOCABULARY:

洗たくをします **sentaku o shimasu** = to do laundry

おうえんします **ōen shimasu** = to cheer

さんぽをします **sanpo o shimasu** = to take a walk

運転します **untenshimasu** = to drive

▪ NOTES ▪

The causative-passive form of します **shimasu** and 来ます **kimasu** (Group 3 verbs) are させられます **saseraremasu** and 来させられます **kosaseraremasu**, respectively.

WRITE THE FOLLOWING IN JAPANESE:

1. I was forced to walk the dog by my mom.

2. I was forced to cheer him by my friend.

3. My younger sister was forced to drive by my older sister.

1. 私は、母に犬のさんぽをさせられました。
2. 私は、友だちにおうえんをさせられました。
3. 姉は、妹に運転させられました。

PHRASE 231

友だち　の　ような　人　と、結婚　したい　です。

Tomodachi no yō na hito to, kekkon shitai desu.

Friend [PART] similar to person [PART] marry want to [COPULA]

= I would like to marry someone who is like my friend.

COPY THE JAPANESE SENTENCE:

VOCABULARY:

結婚します **kekkon shimasu** = to marry

のような **no yō na** = similar to, be like ...

有名人 **yūmeijin** = celebrity

テレビゲーム **terebigēmu** = video games

▪ NOTES ▪

のような **NO YŌ NA** is used when you want to describe something using another noun. It is equivalent to "similar to" or "be like ... ."

WRITE THE FOLLOWING IN JAPANESE:

1. I want to buy a video game, similar to my friend's.

____

____

2. I want to buy clothes, similar to the celebrities'.

____

____

3. I want a dog, similar to my friend's.

____

____

1. 私は、友だちのようなテレビゲームが、買いたいです。
2. 私は、有名人のような洋服が、買いたいです。
3. 私は、友だちのような犬が、ほしいです。

PHRASE 232

私　は、　兄　の　ように　食べています。

Watashi wa, ani no yō ni tabeteimasu.

I [PART] older brother [PART] similar to eating

= I am eating in the same way as my brother's.

COPY THE JAPANESE SENTENCE:

VOCABULARY:

のように **no yō ni** = in the same way, like, just like

忙しい **isogashii** = is busy

うるさい **urusai** = is noisy

混んでいます **kondeimasu** = is crowded

▪ NOTES ▪

This phrases uses the のように **NO YŌ NI** form which is similar to the のような **NO YŌ NA** form. The latter has a noun phrase following directly before のような **no yō na**, whereas のように **no yō ni** has an adjectival or verbal phrase following it.

WRITE THE FOLLOWING IN JAPANESE:

1. My younger brother is noisy, just like my dog.

2. New York is crowded, just like in Tokyo.

3. My younger sister is busy, just like my older sister.

1. 弟は、私の犬のようにうるさいです。
2. ニューヨークは、東京のように混んでいます。
3. 妹は、姉のように忙しいです。

PHRASE 233

父 は、 私 に 姉 の ように 勉強 してほしいです。

Chichi wa, watashi ni ane no yō ni benkyō shite hoshii desu.

My dad [PART] I [PART] my older sister [PART] like study want to do [COPULA]

= My father wants me to study like my older sister.

COPY THE JAPANESE SENTENCE:

VOCABULARY:

がんばります **ganbarimasu** = to do my best

がんばって **ganbatte** = Do your best.

黙ります **damarimasu** = to be quiet

料理します **ryōri shimasu** = to cook

▪ NOTES ▪

This phrase is used when you want to express how you would like someone to do something. Similar to the last two pages, you will put the thing or person that you wanted emulated right before のように... (し)てほしい **no yō ni ... (shi)te hoshii.**

WRITE THE FOLLOWING IN JAPANESE:

1. My mom wants my younger brother to be quiet like my older brother.

2. My dad wants me to cook like a chef.

3. My mom wants me to do my best, just like my younger sister.

1. 母は、弟に兄のように黙ってほしいです。
2. 父は、私にシェフのように料理してほしいです。
3. 母は、私に妹のようにがんばってほしいです。

PHRASE 234

いま　晩ご飯　を　食べた　ばかり　です。

Ima　ban-gohan　o　tabeta　bakari　desu.

Now　dinner　[PART]　ate　have just　[COPULA]

= I have just eaten dinner.

COPY THE JAPANESE SENTENCE:

VOCABULARY:

ばかり **bakari** = have just

入院します **nyūin shimasu** = to be hospitalized

警察 **keisatsu** = police

帰ってきます **kaettekimasu** = to return, to come back

▪ NOTES ▪

The ばかり **BAKARI** form is used to express something that you have just completed.

WRITE THE FOLLOWING IN JAPANESE:

1. The police have just come.

2. I have just come back from Japan.

3. My mom has just got hospitalized.

1. 警察が来たばかりです。
2. 私は、日本から帰ってきたばかりです。
3. 母は、入院したばかりです。

PHRASE 235

日本 に 来て、初めて ハンバーガー を 食べました。

Nihon ni kite, hajimete hanbāgā o tabemashita.

Japan [PART] come first time hamburger [PART] ate

= This is the first time I've eaten a hamburger, after coming to Japan.

COPY THE JAPANESE SENTENCE:

VOCABULARY:

カリフォルニア **Kariforunia** = California

ユタ **Yuta** = Utah

サーフィン **sāfin** = surfing

乗り物 **norimono** = rides

あきます **akimasu** = to get tired of

▪ NOTES ▪

て初めて **TE HAJIMETE** is formed using the て **TE** form of the VERB + 初めて **hajimete**. On this page we will concentrate on Group 3 verbs.

WRITE THE FOLLOWING IN JAPANESE:

1. This is the first time that I rode on the rides, after coming to the amusement park.

____

____

2. This is the first time that I surfed, after coming to California.

____

____

3. This is the first time that I have skiied, after coming to Utah.

____

____

3. ユタに来て、初めてスキーをしました。
2. カリフォルニアに来て、初めてサーフィンをしました。
1. ゆうえん地に来て、初めて乗り物に乗りました。

PHRASE 236

ホットドッグ を 食べて、初めて マスタード を 付けました。

Hottodoggu o tabete, hajimete masutādo o tsukemashita.

Hotdog [PART] eat, the first time mustard [PART] put on

= I put mustard on (eating) a hotdog for the first time.

COPY THE JAPANESE SENTENCE:

____

____

____

VOCABULARY:

マスタード **masutādo** = mustard　えび **ebi** = shrimp

びっくりします **bikkuri shimasu** = to be surprised

好きになります **suki ni narimasu** = to come to like

受けます **ukemasu** = to take (a test)

▪ NOTES ▪

We continue to practice the phrase, て初めて **TE HAJIMETE**, using Group 2 verbs on this page.

WRITE THE FOLLOWING IN JAPANESE:

1. I began to like eating shrimp for the first time.

2. I was surprised, watching the movie for the first time.

3. I was nervous, taking the test for the first time.

1. えびを食べて、初めて好きになりました。
2. 映画を見て、初めてびっくりしました。
3. テストを受けて、初めてドキドキしました。

PHRASE 237

日本 に 来て、初めて 地下鉄 に 乗りました。

Nihon ni kite, hajimete chikatetsu ni norimashita.

Japan [PART] come, the first time subway [PART] to ride on

= After coming to Japan, I rode on a subway for the first time.

COPY THE JAPANESE SENTENCE:

____

____

____

VOCABULARY:

登ります **noborimasu** = to climb

ネパール **Nepāru** = Nepal

マラソン **marason** = marathon

コアラ **koara** = koala

長いきょり **nagai kyori** = long distance

▪ **NOTES** ▪

We continue to practice the phrase, て初めて **TE HAJIMETE.** On this phrase we focus on using this phrase with Group 3 verbs.

WRITE THE FOLLOWING IN JAPANESE:

1. After coming to Nepal, I climbed a mountain for the first time.

____

____

2. Running a marathon, I ran long distance for the first time.

____

____

3. After coming to Australia, I saw a koala for the first time.

____

____

1. ネパールに来て、初めて山を登りました。
2. マラソンして、初めて長いきょりを走りました。
3. オーストラリアに来て、初めてコアラを見ました。

PHRASE 238

私　は、日本　は　すばらしい　と　思います。

Watashi	**wa,**	**Nihon**	**wa**	**subarashii**	**to**	**omoimasu.**
I	[PART]	Japan	[PART]	wonderful	[PART]	think

= I think Japan is wonderful.

COPY THE JAPANESE SENTENCE:

VOCABULARY:

すばらしい **subarashii** = is wonderful

思います **omoimasu** = to think

かっこいい **kakkoii** = is cool, is stylish

美しい **utsukushii** = is beautiful

沖縄 **Okinawa** = Okinawa

▪ NOTES ▪

On this page we focus on using this phrase と思います **to omoimasu** with Group 2 verbs. If it is a な **NA** adjective, you will need to attach the な **NA** adjective with a だ **DA**.

WRITE THE FOLLOWING IN JAPANESE:

1. I think that Okinawa is fun.

2. I think that my dad is cool.

3. I think that the beach is beautiful.

1. 私は、沖縄は楽しいと思います。
2. 私は、父がかっこいいと思います。
3. 私は、海が美しいと思います。

PHRASE 239

ニューヨーク は、自由の女神 で 有名 です。

Nyūyōku wa, jiyū-no-megami de yūmei desu.

New York [PART] Statue of Liberty [PART] famous [COPULA]

= New York is famous for the Statue of Liberty.

COPY THE JAPANESE SENTENCE:

VOCABULARY:

自由の女神 **jiyū-no-megami** = Statue of Liberty

エッフェル塔 **Efferu-tō** = Eiffel Tower

カンガルー **kangarū** = kangaroo

フットボール選手 **futtobōru senshu** = football player

▪ NOTES ▪

This phrase is relatively easy to form. It is: NOUN は **WA** + … で有名です **… de yūmei desu** to say "what it is famous for."

WRITE THE FOLLOWING IN JAPANESE:

1. My older brother is famous as a football player.

2. Australia is famous for its kangaroos.

3. Paris is famous for the Eiffel Tower.

1. 兄は、フットボール選手で有名です。
2. オーストラリアは、カンガルーで有名です。
3. パリは、エッフェル塔で有名です。

PHRASE 240

やっぱり　日本　に　行く　こと　に　しました。

Yappari Nihon ni iku koto ni shimashita.

As planned Japan [PART] go matter [PART] did

= As planned, I have decided to go to Japan.

COPY THE JAPANESE SENTENCE:

VOCABULARY:

やっぱり **yappari** = as planned, as expected, likewise, too

こと **koto** = matter

農場 **nōjō** = farm

郊外 **kōgai** = suburbs

経済 **keizai** = economics

ことにします **koto ni shimasu** = to decide on ~

▪ NOTES ▪

やっぱり **YAPPARI** is used often in everyday speech. It can easily be incorporated in many situations like giving compliments and deciding on a certain plan.

WRITE THE FOLLOWING IN JAPANESE:

1. I too want to live in the suburbs.

2. I too want to study economics.

3. Likewise, I want to go to a farm.

1. やっぱり郊外に住みたいです。
2. やっぱり経済を勉強したいです。
3. やっぱり農場に行きたいです。

PHRASE 241

なるべく　静か　に　して　ください。

Narubeku　shizuka　ni　shite　kudasai.

As much as possible　quiet　[PART]　to do　please

= As much as you can, please be quiet.

COPY THE JAPANESE SENTENCE:

VOCABULARY:

なるべく **narubeku** = as much as possible

けんこうにいい **kenkō ni ii** = is healthy

物 **mono** = thing

▪ NOTES ▪

なるべく **NARUBEKU** is a great way to start a sentence to tell someone what he/she should do. You will often hear a parent use this phrase as part of what they expect their child(ren) to do.

WRITE THE FOLLOWING IN JAPANESE:

1. As much as you can, please eat healthy things.

____

____

2. As much as you can, please sleep early.

____

____

3. As much as you can, please drink a lot of water.

____

____

1. なるべくけんこうにいい物を、食べてください。
2. なるべく早く寝てください。
3. なるべくたくさん水を、飲んでください。

PHRASE 242

なかなか　病気　が　なおりません。

Nakanaka　byōki　ga　naorimasen.

Not readily　illness　[PART]　not get better

= I'm not getting any better from my illness.

COPY THE JAPANESE SENTENCE:

___

___

___

VOCABULARY:

なかなか **nakanaka** = not easily, not readily

なおります **naorimasu** = to get better

時 **toki** = when

食欲がでます **shokuyoku ga demasu** = to have an appetite

▪ **NOTES** ▪

なかなか **NAKANAKA** in a phrase is used to mean "not easily, not readily" and the sentence has a negative verb ending.

WRITE THE FOLLOWING IN JAPANESE:

1. Not easily do I have an appetite.

2. I do not win easily.

3. I am not able to buy a car easily.

1. なかなか食欲がでません。
2. なかなか勝てません。
3. なかなか車が買えません。

PHRASE 243

私　は、家族　の　ため　に、たくさん 働いています。

Watashi wa, kazoku no tame ni, takusan hataraiteimasu.

I [PART] my family [PART] for [PART] a lot working

= I work a lot for (the sake of) my family.

COPY THE JAPANESE SENTENCE:

VOCABULARY:

のために **no tame ni** = for (the purpose/sake of)

働きます **hatarakimasu** = to work

教育 **kyōiku** = education

おもちゃ **omocha** = toy

仕事 **shigoto** = business

▪ NOTES ▪

In this phrase, のために **NO TAME NI** "for the purpose/sake of" is preceded by a NOUN + の **NO**. That noun is the person or thing that the action is done for.

WRITE THE FOLLOWING IN JAPANESE:

1. I study a lot for (the purpose of) education.

2. I bought this toy for (the sake of) my son.

3. I am going to China for (the sake of) business.

1. 教育のために、たくさん勉強します。
2. 息子のために、おもちゃを買いました。
3. 仕事のために、中国に行きます。

PHRASE 244

この　皿　は、とても　日本的　です。

Kono sara wa, totemo Nihon-teki desu.

This plate [PART] very Japanese-like [COPULA]

= This plate is very Japanese (in design).

COPY THE JAPANESE SENTENCE:

VOCABULARY:

的 **teki** = -ish, -like

絵 **e** = painting

言葉 **kotoba** = words

いす **isu** = chair

▪ NOTES ▪

的 **TEKI** is attached to nouns to mean "-ish" or "-like" in English.

WRITE THE FOLLOWING IN JAPANESE:

1. The words are very French (in sounds).

2. The chair is very Italian (in looks).

3. The food is Chinese (in taste).

1. その言葉は、とてもフランス的です。
2. そのいすは、とてもイタリア的です。
3. その食べ物は、中国的です。

PHRASE 245

ステーキ ばかり 食べる のは、けんこうに わるいです。

Sutēki	**bakari**	**taberu**	**no wa,**	**kenkō**	**ni**	**warui**	**desu.**
Steak	only	to eat	[PART]	health	[PART]	bad	[COPULA]

= Eating only steak is not good for your health.

COPY THE JAPANESE SENTENCE:

VOCABULARY:

けんこうにわるい **kenkō ni warui** = is unhealthy

ばかり **bakari** = only

目にわるい **me ni warui** = is bad for the eyes

ビール **bīru** = beer

▪ NOTES ▪

For this phrase, the ばかり **bakari** comes directly after the NOUN. The noun is the object of one's sole or habitual action. The result of one's action is given in the second half of the sentence.

WRITE THE FOLLOWING IN JAPANESE:

1. Drinking only beer is not good for your health.

____

____

2. Playing only video games is bad for your eyes.

____

____

3. Eating only snacks is unhealthy.

____

____

1. ビールばかり飲むのは、けんこうにわるいです。
2. テレビゲームばかりするのは、目にわるいです。
3. おかしばかり食べるのは、けんこうにわるいです。

PHRASE 246

テニス を 始める こと に しました。

Tenisu o hajimeru koto ni shimashita.

Tennis [PART] to start resolve [PART] did

= I have decided to start playing tennis.

COPY THE JAPANESE SENTENCE:

VOCABULARY:

始めます **hajimemasu** = to start

あみ物 **amimono** = knitting

ラテン語 **Raten-go** = Latin

運動 **undō** = exercise

▪ NOTES ▪

The phrase VERB/NOUN + 始めることにしました **HAJIMERU KOTO ni shimashita** expresses the idea that someone has decided to do something or has started to do something. The VERB/NOUN is expressed before the 始めることにします **hajimeru koto ni shimasu** phrase.

WRITE THE FOLLOWING IN JAPANESE:

1. I have decided to start exercising.

2. I have decided to start learning Latin.

3. My grandmother has decided to start knitting.

1. 私は、運動を始めることにしました。
2. 私は、ラテン語の勉強を始めることにしました。
3. おばあさんは、あみ物を始めることにしました。

PHRASE 247

ドア を 開けた まま 出かけました。

Doa o aketa mama dekakemashita.

Door [PART] opened leaving went out

= Leaving the door open, I went out of the house.

COPY THE JAPANESE SENTENCE:

VOCABULARY:

まま **mama** = as it is, leaving it

出かけます **dekakemasu** = to go out of the house

ヒーター **hītā** = heater

エアコン **eakon** = air conditioning

▪ NOTES ▪

まま **MAMA** is used to give the idea that you left something that should have been completed and did something else. There is usually a feeling of not being in the right state of mind.

WRITE THE FOLLOWING IN JAPANESE:

1. Leaving the heater on, I went to the supermarket.

2. Leaving the air conditioner on, I went to school.

3. Leaving the TV on, I slept.

1. ヒーターをつけたまま、スーパーへ行きました。
2. エアコンをつけたまま、学校に行きました。
3. テレビをつけたまま、寝ました。

PHRASE 248

姉　は、ねつ　で　顔　が　赤っぽい　です。

Ane wa, netsu de kao ga akappoi desu.

My older sister [PART] fever [PART] face [PART] looks red [COPULA]

= My older sister has a fever and her face looks red.

COPY THE JAPANESE SENTENCE:

VOCABULARY:

っぽい **ppoi** = seems like

安っぽい **yasppoi** = is cheap

黒っぽい **kuroppoi** = is black

ねつ **netsu** = fever

うそっぽい **usoppoi** = is false

顔 **kao** = face

▪ NOTES ▪

っぽい **PPOI** is attached to a noun or an adjective to mean "-ish" or "is like."

WRITE THE FOLLOWING IN JAPANESE:

1. My younger brother's laptop seems cheap.

2. My pants seems black.

3. That story seems like a false story.

1. 弟のラップトップは、安っぽいです。
2. 私のズボンは、黒っぽいです。
3. あの話は、うそっぽいです。

PHRASE 249

父　は、おこりっぽい です。

Chichi　wa,　okorippoi　desu.

My father [PART]　short temper　[COPULA] = My father is short-tempered.

COPY THE JAPANESE SENTENCE:

VOCABULARY:

おこりっぽい **okorippoi** = is short-tempered

忘れっぽい **wasureppoi** = is forgetful

白っぽい **shiroppoi** = is whitish

あきっぽい **akippoi** = is easily bored

▪ NOTES ▪

This page continues with the っぽい **PPOI** form, used here to describe some characteristics of a person or thing.

WRITE THE FOLLOWING IN JAPANESE:

1. My mother is always forgetful.

2. Our child is easily bored.

3. I like the whitish one.

1. 母は、いつも忘れっぽいです。
2. うちの子どもは、あきっぽいです。
3. 私は、白っぽいのが好きです。

PHRASE 250

仕事 を すれば、する ほど 仕事 が ふえます。

Shigoto o sure ba, suru hodo shigoto ga fuemasu.

Job	[PART]	if do	to do	than	job	[PART]	increase

= The more work I do, the more it increases.

COPY THE JAPANESE SENTENCE:

VOCABULARY:

すれば、するほど **sure ba, suru hodo** = more ~ the more

ふえます **fuemasu** = to increase

わかります **wakarimasu** = to understand

たいじゅう **taijū** = weight

遠い **tōi** = is far

▪ NOTES ▪

すれば、するほど **sure ba, suru hodo** phrase is used to express the idea that "the more you do something, something else happens."

WRITE THE FOLLOWING IN JAPANESE:

1. The more I study, the less I understand.

2. The more I exercise, the more I gain weight.

3. The more I drive, the farther it gets.

1. 勉強すれば、するほどわからなくなります。
2. 運動すれば、するほど体重が増えます。
3. 運転すれば、するほど遠くなります。

PHRASE 251

一万円　さえ　あれ　ば、この　ゲーム　が　買えます。

Ichiman-en sae are ba, kono gēmu ga kaemasu.

10,000 yen at the least have if this game [PART] able to buy

= If I had at least 10,000 yen, I would be able to buy this game.

COPY THE JAPANESE SENTENCE:

VOCABULARY:

ゲーム **gēmu** = game

二時間 **ni-jikan** = two hours

満点 **manten** = perfect score

とります **torimasu** = to get

▪ NOTES ▪

This phrase uses several grammar points that we've learned previously: the ば **BA** form for the "if" form, and the potential form for the verb ending at the end of the sentence.

WRITE THE FOLLOWING IN JAPANESE:

1. If I study for just two hours, I can get a perfect score.

2. If I have at least 5,000 yen, I can eat for one week.

3. I am happy if I can just drink water.

1. 二時間勉強すれば、満点をとれます。
2. 五千円あれば、一週間食べられます。
3. 水さえ飲めれば、うれしいです。

PHRASE 252

一体、 どこ に 行きましたか。

Ittai, doko ni ikimashita ka.

What the heck, where [PART] went [question form]

= Where in the world did you go?

COPY THE JAPANESE SENTENCE:

VOCABULARY:

一体 **ittai** = where in the world, what the heck

考えます **kangaemasu** = to think

食堂 **shokudō** = dining hall

泳ぎます **oyogimasu** = to swim

▪ NOTES ▪

You can use this phrase when you are confused and would like an answer. You can hear this being used by parents when they question their son or daughter for doing something in particular.

WRITE THE FOLLOWING IN JAPANESE:

1. What in the world did you eat at the dining hall?

____

____

2. What in the world are you thinking?

____

____

3. Where in the world did you swim?

____

____

1. 一体、食堂で何を食べましたか。
2. 一体、何を考えていますか。
3. 一体、どこで泳ぎましたか。

PHRASE 253

私　は、一ヶ月　で　日本　に　なれました。

Watashi wa, ik-kagetsu de Nihon ni naremashita.

I [PART] one month [PART] Japan [PART] to get used to

= In a month, I got used to Japan.

COPY THE JAPANESE SENTENCE:

VOCABULARY:

なれます **naremasu** = to get used to

義理のお母さん **giri no okāsan** = step-mother

イタリア語 **Itaria-go** = Italian language

納豆 **nattō** = fermented soy beans

▪ NOTES ▪

This phrase is straightforward. You will put the noun right before になれます **ni naremasu**.

WRITE THE FOLLOWING IN JAPANESE:

1. In a week, I got used to Italian (language).

____

____

2. Last week, I got used to fermented soy beans.

____

____

3. This year, I got used to my step-mother.

____

____

1. 一週間で、私はイタリア語になれました。
2. 先週、私は納豆になれました。
3. 今年、義理のお母さんになれました。

PHRASE 254

学校 が ない うち に、旅行 に 行きます。

Gakkō ga nai uchi ni ryokō ni ikimasu.

School [PART] none when [PART] travel [PART] to go

= I will go on a trip when I don't have school.

COPY THE JAPANESE SENTENCE:

VOCABULARY:

うちに **uchi ni** = while, during, when

ない **nai** = none, not (have)

動物園 **dōbutsuen** = zoo

アルバイトをします **arubaito o shimasu** = to work a part-time job

▪ NOTES ▪

This phrase uses the word うちに **UCHI NI** which means "while." Please notice that the word ない **nai** "not" comes before うちに **uchi ni.**

WRITE THE FOLLOWING IN JAPANESE:

1. When I don't have to work, I will go to the zoo.

2. When I don't have school, I will work a part-time job.

3. When I don't have to work, I will go to South Korea.

1. 仕事がないうちに、動物園へ行きます。
2. 学校がないうちに、アルバイトをします。
3. 仕事がないうちに、かん国に行きます。

PHRASE 255

車　に　気を付けて　ください。

Kuruma　ni　ki o tsukete　kudasai.

Car [PART] be careful please = Please look out for the cars.

COPY THE JAPANESE SENTENCE:

VOCABULARY:

気を付けます **ki o tsukemasu** = to be cautious, to pay attention

かいだん **daidan** = stairs

ナイフ **naifu** = knife

油 **abura** = oil

▪ NOTES ▪

This is a very useful phrase. You will often hear this phrase used by others to tell you to watch out for something. The phrase is also easy to form. You will just need to put the noun before に気を付けます **ni ki o tsukemasu**.

WRITE THE FOLLOWING IN JAPANESE:

1. Please look out for the stairs.

____

____

2. Pay attention to the hot oil.

____

____

3. Be careful of the knife.

____

____

1. かいだんに、気を付けてください。
2. 熱い油に、気を付けてください。
3. ナイフに、気を付けてください。

PHRASE 256

子ども　の　くせに　なまいき　です　ね。

Kodomo no kuse ni namaiki desu ne.

Child [PART] in spite of cheeky [PART] aren't you

= You are cheeky for a child. (Although you're a child, you are cheeky.)

COPY THE JAPANESE SENTENCE:

VOCABULARY:

くせに **kuse ni** = in spite of, although

なまいき **namaiki** = is cheeky

してはいけません **shite wa ikemasen** = must not (do)

けがをします **kega o shimasu** = to get injured

二さい **nisai** = two years old

おとな **otona** = adult

▪ NOTES ▪

くせに **KUSE NI** "in spite of, though" is used when you think somebody oversteps their boundaries. It is usually not said as a compliment.

WRITE THE FOLLOWING IN JAPANESE:

1. Although he got injured, he wanted to go for a walk.

2. Although the child is two years old, he wants to drink coffee.

3. Even though you are an adult, you must not do this.

3. おとなのくせに、こんなことをしてはいけません。
2. 二さいの子どものくせに、コーヒーを飲みたがります。
1. 彼はけがをしたくせに、さんぽをしたがりました。

PHRASE 257

悪い　てんすう　が　気になります。

Warui　　tensū　　ga　　ki ni narimasu.

Poor　　scores　　[PART]　　to be concerned

= I am concerned about my poor scores.

COPY THE JAPANESE SENTENCE:

VOCABULARY:

てんすう **tensū** = score

けが **kega** = injury

くぎ **kugi** = nail (like a screw)

さびた **sabita** = is rusty

気になります **ki ni narimasu** = to be concerned

▪ NOTES ▪

気になります **KI NI NARIMASU** is used when you want to express something that bothers or concerns you.

WRITE THE FOLLOWING IN JAPANESE:

1. I am concerned about the rusty nail.

____

____

2. I am concerned about your injury.

____

____

3. I am concerned about the weather tomorrow.

____

____

1. さびたくぎが、気になります。
2. あなたのけがが、気になります。
3. 明日の天気が、気になります。

PHRASE 258

私　は、しゅっちょう　で　日本　へ　行きます。

Watashi wa, shucchō de Nihon e ikimasu.

I [PART] business trip [PART] Japan to to go

= I will go to Japan on a business trip.

COPY THE JAPANESE SENTENCE:

VOCABULARY:

しゅっちょう **shucchō** = business trip

ブラジル **Burajiru** = Brazil

シカゴ **Shikago** = Chicago

ボストン **Bosuton** = Boston

▪ NOTES ▪

Like many workers in developed countries, Japanese workers often go on business trips domestically and internationally. If you work for an international company, business trips can be quite frequent.

WRITE THE FOLLOWING IN JAPANESE:

1. I will go to Chicago on a business trip.

2. My dad will go to Boston on a business trip.

3. My mom will go to Brazil on a business trip.

1. 私は、しゅっちょうでシカゴへ行きます。
2. 父は、しゅっちょうでボストンへ行きます。
3. 母は、しゅっちょうでブラジルへ行きます。

PHRASE 259

私　は、毎日　テニス　を　練習します。

Watashi wa, mainichi tenisu o renshū shimasu.

I [PART] every day tennis [PART] to practice

= I practice tennis every day.

COPY THE JAPANESE SENTENCE:

VOCABULARY:

ラグビー **ragubī** = rugby

サッカー **sakkā** = soccer

アメフト **Amefuto** = American football

たいてい **taitei** = usually

▪ NOTES ▪

In Japanese, アメフト **Amefuto** refers to American football, and サッカー **sakkā** to American soccer.

WRITE THE FOLLOWING IN JAPANESE:

1. I practice soccer every day.

2. I usually practice football.

3. I practice rugby every day.

1. 私は、毎日サッカーを練習します。
2. 私は、たいていアメフトを練習します。
3. 私は、毎日ラグビーを練習します。

PHRASE 260

ハンバーガー は、ホットドッグ ほど おいしくない です。

Hanbāgā	**wa,**	**hottodoggu**	**hodo**	**oishikunai**	**desu.**
Hamburger	[PART]	hotdog	not as much	not delicious	[COPULA]

= Hamburgers are not as delicious as hotdogs.

COPY THE JAPANESE SENTENCE:

VOCABULARY:

ほど **hodo** = not as much

やさしい **yasashii** = is nice

きびしい **kibishii** = is strict

おとなしい **otonashii** = is quiet

▪ **NOTES** ▪

The ほど **HODO** form is used to express that something is not as ADJECTIVE as another noun. For this phrase, the adjective must be in the negative form. On this page, we will focus on い **I** adjectives.

WRITE THE FOLLOWING IN JAPANESE:

1. Tom is not as nice as Jim.

2. Ms. Tanaka is not as strict as Ms. Sato.

3. My son is not as quiet as my daughter.

1. トムは、ジムほどやさしくないです。
2. 田中さんは、佐藤さんほどきびしくないです。
3. 息子は、娘ほどおとなしくないです。

PHRASE 261

私　の　友だち　に　よると、　明日　は　学校　が　ありません。

Watashi no tomodachi ni yoru to, ashita wa gakkō ga arimasen.

I [PART] friend [PART] according to tomorrow [PART] school [PART] there is not

= According to my friend, there won't be school tomorrow.

COPY THE JAPANESE SENTENCE:

VOCABULARY:

によると **ni yoru to** = according to

星 **hoshi** = star

クイズ **kuizu** = quiz

むずかしい **muzukashii** = is difficult

発見されます **hakkensaremasu** = to be discovered

▪ NOTES ▪

The によると **NI YORU TO** form can be used to express that according to someone else, the following is the information. In order to form this sentence structure, you will need to put the person before, and the information after, the phrase によると **ni yoru to.**

WRITE THE FOLLOWING IN JAPANESE:

1. According to the teacher, the quiz will be difficult.

2. According to the newspaper, a new star was discovered yesterday.

3. According to my mom, it will rain tomorrow.

1. 先生によると、クイズはむずかしいです。
2. 新聞によると、昨日新しい星が発見されました。
3. 母によると、明日は雨です。

PHRASE 262

私　は、　今月　二万円　しか　ない　です。

Watashi wa, kongetsu niman-en shika nai desu.

I [PART] this month 20,000 yen only none [COPULA]

= This month, I only have 20,000 yen.

COPY THE JAPANESE SENTENCE:

VOCABULARY:

しかない **shika nai** = only have

今月 **kongetsu** = this month

今週 **konshū** = this week

兄弟 **kyōdai** = sibling

▪ NOTES ▪

In this phrase, you will need to put information about the item that you have before しか **shika**, then followed by ないです **nai desu**.

WRITE THE FOLLOWING IN JAPANESE:

1. I only have two tests this week.

2. I only have one set of homework today.

3. I only have one sibling.

1. 私は、今週しけんが二つしかないです。
2. 私は、今日宿題が一つしかないです。
3. 私は、兄弟が一人しかいないです。

PHRASE 263

私 は、病気 の 時 おかゆ しか 食べません。

Watashi wa, byōki no toki okayu shika tabemasen.

I [PART] sick [PART] time porridge only not eat

= When I am sick, I eat only porridge.

COPY THE JAPANESE SENTENCE:

____

____

____

VOCABULARY:

おかゆ **okayu** = porridge

夏 **natsu** = summer

スポーツドリンク **supōtsu dorinku** = sports drink

試験 **shiken** = exam, examination

あいだ **aida** = during

▪ NOTES ▪

This phrase is very similar to the previous one. On this page, we are including a negative verb at the end of the sentence to mean "When … I only VERB."

WRITE THE FOLLOWING IN JAPANESE:

1. I drink only sports drink when I practice.

2. I study only during the exam.

3. I drink only water in the summer.

1. 練習の時は、スポーツドリンクしか飲みません。
2. 試験のあいだは、勉強しかしません。
3. 夏は、水しか飲みません。

PHRASE 264

明日　は、いよいよ　日本　です　ね。

Ashita wa, iyoiyo Nihon desu ne.

Tomorrow [PART] at last Japan [COPULA] [CONFIRMATION]

= Tomorrow is finally the day for Japan, right?

COPY THE JAPANESE SENTENCE:

VOCABULARY:

いよいよ **iyoiyo** = at last, finally

大学 **daigaku** = college

結婚します **kekkon shimasu** = to marry, to get married

出産します **shussan shimasu** = to deliver a baby

▪ NOTES ▪

いよいよ **IYOIYO** is used to express something that you have been waiting for a while. It connotes some excitement.

WRITE THE FOLLOWING IN JAPANESE:

1. Tomorrow is finally the day for the delivery of my baby.

2. Next week is finally the day for college.

3. My son will finally get married.

1. 明日は、いよいよ出産します。
2. 来週は、いよいよ大学です。
3. 息子は、いよいよ結婚します。

PHRASE 265

娘　は、いつの間にか　おとな　に　なりました。

Musume **wa,** **itsu no ma ni ka** **otona** **ni** **narimashita.**

My daughter [PART] before one knows adult [PART] became

= Before I knew it, my daughter became an adult.

COPY THE JAPANESE SENTENCE:

VOCABULARY:

いつの間にか **itsu no ma ni ka** = before one knows it

亡くなります **nakunarimasu** = to pass away

まご **mago** = grandchild

大学生 **daigakusei** = college student

アップルパイ **appurupai** = apple pie

▪ NOTES ▪

いつの間にか **ITSU NO MA NI KA** is a very useful phrase when you think that something has happened in the blink of an eye. 亡くなります **Nakunarimasu** is the polite form of 死にます **shinimasu**.

WRITE THE FOLLOWING IN JAPANESE:

1. Before I knew it, my grandchild was a college student.

____

____

2. Before I knew it, my grandmother passed away.

____

____

3. Before I knew it, my older brother (completely) ate the apple pie.

____

____

1. まごは、いつの間にか大学生でした。
2. おばあさんは、いつの間にかなくなりました。
3. 兄は、いつの間にかアップルパイを食べてしまいました。

PHRASE 266

この おすし は おいしい ので、たくさん 食べて ください。

Kono	**o-sushi**	**wa**	**oishii**	**no de,**	**takusan**	**tabete**	**kudasai.**
This	sushi	[PART]	delicious	so	a lot	eat	please

= This sushi is delicious so please eat a lot of it.

COPY THE JAPANESE SENTENCE:

VOCABULARY:

ので **no de** = because, so

お茶 **o-cha** = green tea

勝ちます **kachimasu** = to win

強い **tsuyoi** = is strong

▪ **NOTES** ▪

ので **NO DE** is very similar to から **kara** which you have learned previously. ので **NO DE** is a bit more forceful (in the idea given) than から **kara**.

WRITE THE FOLLOWING IN JAPANESE:

1. Because it is cold, I want to drink tea.

____

____

2. Because my team is strong, I think we will win.

____

____

3. Because my scores are good, I am happy.

____

____

1. 寒いので、お茶が飲みたいです。
2. 私たちのチームは強いので、勝つと思います。
3. てんすうがいいので、うれしいです。

PHRASE 267

せっかく 来た ので、一緒 に 食べましょう。

Sekkaku kita no de, issho ni tabemashō.

With trouble came so together [PART] let's eat

= Because I have come (with great effort), let's eat together.

COPY THE JAPANESE SENTENCE:

VOCABULARY:

せっかく **sekkaku** = with great trouble

作ります **tsukurimasu** = to make

浅草 **Asakusa** = Asakusa district

コロシアム **Koroshiamu** = Colosseum

▪ NOTES ▪

せっかく **SEKKAKU** is used to express that one has gone through great efforts to accomplish something. There is no particle after せっかく **sekkaku**.

WRITE THE FOLLOWING IN JAPANESE:

1. Because I went through the trouble of making dinner, please eat.

2. Because we came all the way to Tokyo, let's go to Asakusa.

3. Because we came all the way to Rome, let's see the Colosseum.

1. せっかく晩ご飯を作ったので、食べてください。
2. せっかく東京に来たので、浅草に行きましょう。
3. せっかくローマに来たので、コロシアムを見ましょう。

PHRASE 268

私　は、宿題　が　出るとは、思わなかった です。

Watashi wa, shukudai ga deru to wa, omowanakatta desu.

I [PART] homework [PART] come out [PART] didn't think [COPULA]

= I didn't think that we would get homework.

COPY THE JAPANESE SENTENCE:

VOCABULARY:

出ます **demasu** = to come out

思わなかった **omowanakatta** = didn't think

今年 **kotoshi** = this year

ふぐ **fugu** = blowfish (a delicacy in Japan)

▪ NOTES ▪

The 思わなかった **omowanakatta** phrase is a useful one when something happens unexpectedly. This phrase is easy to construct as you put the first part of the sentence in informal form, followed by とは、思わなかったです **to wa, omowanakatta desu**.

WRITE THE FOLLOWING IN JAPANESE:

1. I didn't think that I would be able to go to Japan this year.

____

____

2. I didn't think that I would be able to eat blowfish.

____

____

3. I didn't think that I would become a college student.

____

____

1. 私は、今年日本へ行けるとは、思わなかったです。
2. 私は、ふぐが食べられるとは、思わなかったです。
3. 私は、大学生になれるとは、思わなかったです。

PHRASE 269

急に 止まらない で ください。

Kyū ni tomaranai de kudasai.

Suddenly don't stop [PART] please = Please don't stop suddenly.

COPY THE JAPANESE SENTENCE:

VOCABULARY:

急に **kyū ni** = suddenly

止まります **tomarimasu** = to stop

さけびます **sakebimasu** = to scream

飛びます **tobimasu** = to jump

▪ NOTES ▪

急に **KYŪ NI** is used to express something that has happened suddenly. As seen above, it is an easy expression to use.

WRITE THE FOLLOWING IN JAPANESE:

1. Please do not scream suddenly.

2. My younger brother jumped suddenly.

3. My younger sister spoke suddenly.

1. 急にさけばないでください。
2. 弟は、急に飛びました。
3. 妹は、急に話しました。

PHRASE 270

まさか　急に ぶつかる とは、思わなかった です。

Masaka kyū ni butsukaru to wa, omowanakatta desu.

Certainly not suddenly crash [PART] didn't think [COPULA]

= I didn't expect that it will crash suddenly.

COPY THE JAPANESE SENTENCE:

VOCABULARY:

まさか **masaka** = certainly not, absolutely not

まさか～とは、思わない **masaka ~ to wa, omowanai** = not expect

フィジー **Fijī** = Fiji

取ります **torimasu** = to get

▪ NOTES ▪

This phrase まさか **masaka** is used to express something that came at a surprise. It is easy to form as you will just need to put まさか **masaka** at the beginning of the sentence.

WRITE THE FOLLOWING IN JAPANESE:

1. I didn't expect that I would be able to go to Fiji.

____

____

2. I didn't expect that I would get a good score.

____

____

3. I didn't expect that I would be able to meet my uncle.

____

____

1. まさかフィジーへ行けるとは、思わなかったです。
2. まさかいい点数を取れるとは、思わなかったです。
3. まさかおじさんに会えるとは、思わなかったです。

PHRASE 271

昨日　は　会ぎ　で、パーティー　に　行けません　でした。

Kinō wa kaigi de, pātī ni ikemasen deshita.

Yesterday [PART] meeting [PART] party [PART] couldn't go [COPULA PAST]

= Because of a meeting, I couldn't go to the party yesterday.

COPY THE JAPANESE SENTENCE:

VOCABULARY:

会ぎ **kaigi** = meeting

目ざまし時計 **mezamashi dokei** = alarm clock

出張 **shucchō** = business trip

そう式 **sōshiki** = funeral

▪ NOTES ▪

The で **DE** in this phrase is preceded by a reason why something occurred. The result is stated after the で **de**.

WRITE THE FOLLOWING IN JAPANESE:

1. Because of a business trip, I will go to South Korea.

____

____

2. Because of the alarm clock, I woke up early.

____

____

3. Because of a funeral, I won't be able to go to school.

____

____

1. 出張で、かん国に行きます。
2. 目覚まし時計で、早く起きました。
3. そう式で、学校へ行けません。

PHRASE 272

明日　は　テスト　が　ある　ような気がします。

Ashita　wa　testo　ga　aru　yō na ki ga shimasu.

Tomorrow [PART]　test　[PART] there is　have a feeling

= I have a feeling that there is a test tomorrow.

COPY THE JAPANESE SENTENCE:

VOCABULARY:

ような気がします **yō na ki ga shimasu** = have a feeling

高い **takai** = is expensive

亀 **kame** = turtle

体に悪い **karada ni warui** = bad for your body

年をとっている **toshi o totteiru** = is old

▪ NOTES ▪

This phrase ような気がします **yō na ki ga shimasu** is used to express your feeling about something. As you can see in the above example, it is easy to form.

WRITE THE FOLLOWING IN JAPANESE:

1. I feel that this drink is bad for your body.

2. I feel that this turtle is old.

3. I feel that this car will be expensive.

1. この飲み物は、体に悪いような気がします。
2. この亀は、年をとっているような気がします。
3. この車は、高いような気がします。

PHRASE 273

コーラ と スプライト で、どちら が 好き ですか。

Kōra	to	Supuraito	de	dochira	ga	suki	desu ka.
Cola	[PART]	Sprite	[PART]	which one	[PART]	like	[COPULA QUESTION]

= Between cola and sprite, which one do you like better?

COPY THE JAPANESE SENTENCE:

VOCABULARY:

どちら **dochira** = which one

方 **hō** = more than

パン **pan** = bread

早い **hayai** = is fast

電車 **densha** = electric train

▪ NOTES ▪

どちら **DOCHIRA** is used to ask questions to compare two things. If you follow the pattern above, it is quite easy to construct this type of questions.

WRITE THE FOLLOWING IN JAPANESE:

1. Between bread and cooked rice, which one do you like more?

2. Between a car and an electric train, which one is faster?

3. Between Japanese and English, which one is more difficult?

1. パンとご飯で、どちらが好きですか。
2. 車と電車で、どちらが早いですか。
3. 日本語と英語で、どちらがむずかしいですか。

PHRASE 274

私 は、明日 の 朝 もっと 勉強 します。

Watashi wa, ashita no asa motto benkyō shimasu.

I [PART] tomorrow [PART] morning more study to do

= I will study more tomorrow morning.

COPY THE JAPANESE SENTENCE:

VOCABULARY:

もっと **motto** = more

がんばります **ganbarimasu** = try hard

たまごやき **tamagoyaki** = grilled eggs for sushi

ジュース **jūsu** = juice

▪ NOTES ▪

もっと **MOTTO** is a useful word to know in Japanese. You can use it as a standalone word in informal situations to mean simply "more." The above example shows how it is used in a sentence.

WRITE THE FOLLOWING IN JAPANESE:

1. I want to drink more juice.

---

2. I will try harder.

---

3. My mom wants to eat more grilled eggs for sushi.

---

1. 私は、もっとジュースが飲みたいです。
2. 私は、もっとがんばります。
3. 母は、もっとたまごやきが食べたいです。

PHRASE 275

今 から、テニス に ついて 話します。

Ima kara, tenisu ni tsuite hanashimasu.

Now from tennis [PART] about to speak

= I will speak about tennis from now.

COPY THE JAPANESE SENTENCE:

VOCABULARY:

について **ni tsuite** = about, concerning

桜 **sakura** = cherry blossoms

政府 **seifu** = government

馬 **uma** = horse

▪ NOTES ▪

について **NI TSUITE** is often used when you want to talk about a certain topic. It can set the topic so that the audience knows what you will be talking about. This phrase is easy to form: just put the noun before について **ni tsuite**. Finish the sentence by saying 書きます **kakimasu** or 話します **hanashimasu** or any other verb that makes sense.

WRITE THE FOLLOWING IN JAPANESE:

1. I will be writing about the government.

2. I will be talking about horses.

3. I will be writing about cherry blossoms.

1. 政府について書きます。
2. 馬について話します。
3. 桜について書きます。

PHRASE 276

雪　の　せい　で、学校　は　ありません。

Yuki　no　sei　de,　gakkō　wa　arimasen.

Snow [PART] due to [PART] school [PART] not have

= Because of the snow, we don't have school.

COPY THE JAPANESE SENTENCE:

VOCABULARY:

せい **sei** = because of, due to

不景気 **fukeiki** = bad economy

遅れます **okuremasu** = to be late

かみなり **kaminari** = thunderstorms

飛びます **tobimasu** = to fly

▪ NOTES ▪

せい **SEI** is used to mean "due to" or "because of." This phrase is used when the result is something undesirable.

WRITE THE FOLLOWING IN JAPANESE:

1. Because of the bad economy, this year is difficult.

2. Because of my younger brother, we are late.

3. Because of the thunderstorms, the airplane didn't fly.

1. 不景気のせいで、今年は大変です。
2. 弟のせいで、遅れました。
3. かみなりのせいで、飛行機は飛びませんでした。

PHRASE 277

私　は、せめて 九十点　は とりたい です。

Watashi wa, semete kyūjut-ten wa toritai desu.

I [PART] at least 90 points [PART] want to get [COPULA]

= I want to get at least 90 points.

COPY THE JAPANESE SENTENCE:

VOCABULARY:

せめて **semete** = at least

必要です **hitsuyō desu** = to need

寝袋 **nebukuro** = sleeping bag

▪ **NOTES** ▪

せめて **SEMETE** is an easy word to include in your sentence when needed, to emphasize the minimal amount that is needed.

WRITE THE FOLLOWING IN JAPANESE:

1. I will need at least a sleeping bag for camping.

2. I will need at least a pencil at school.

3. I will take at least water.

1. キャンプでは、せめて寝袋が必要です。
2. 学校では、せめてえんぴつが必要です。
3. 私は、せめて水を持って行きます。

PHRASE 278

私 は、ゴルフ が 好き です が、へた です。

Watashi wa, gorufu ga suki desu ga, heta desu.

I [PART] golf [PART] like [COPULA] but unskillful [COPULA]

= I like golf but I am not skillful at it.

COPY THE JAPANESE SENTENCE:

VOCABULARY:

が **ga** = but, however

長い **nagai** = is long

面白い **omoshiroi** = is interesting

抹茶 **maccha** = ceremonial green tea

▪ NOTES ▪

が **GA** is used as a conjunction here, to mean "but." It joins two sentences into a more complex sentence.

WRITE THE FOLLOWING IN JAPANESE:

1. The movie was interesting but long.

2. I am unskillful at tennis but I like it.

3. I went to Japan but I did not drink ceremonial green tea.

1. 映画は面白かったですが、長かったです。
2. 私は、テニスがへたですが、好きです。
3. 私は、日本へ行きましたが、抹茶を飲みませんでした。

PHRASE 279

うち　の　窓　から、山　が　見えます。

Uchi no mado kara, yama ga miemasu.

My house [PART] window from mountain [PART] can see

= I can see the mountain from my window.

COPY THE JAPANESE SENTENCE:

VOCABULARY:

見えます **miemasu** = can see

雲 **kumo** = cloud

黒板 **kokuban** = blackboard

建物 **tatemono** = building

▪ **NOTES** ▪

みえます **MIEMASU** is used to express what you are able to see. This phrase is easy to form as you put the noun before みえます **miemasu** and connect it with the particle が **GA**.

WRITE THE FOLLOWING IN JAPANESE:

1. I can see the clouds from the window.

2. I cannot see the blackboard from my desk.

3. I can see the buildings from the airplane.

1. 窓から雲が見えます。
2. 私のつくえから黒板が見えません。
3. 飛行機から建物が見えます。

PHRASE 280

この　すきやき　は、けっこう　おいしい　です　ね。

Kono　sukiyaki　wa,　kekkō　oishii　desu　ne.

This　sukiyaki　[PART]　quite　delicious　[COPULA] isn't it

= This sukiyaki is quite delicious, isn't it?

COPY THE JAPANESE SENTENCE:

VOCABULARY:

けっこう **kekkō** = quite, rather, reasonably

おいしい **oishii** = is delicious

頭がいい **atama ga ii** = is smart

今年の夏 **kotoshi no natsu** = this summer

涼しい **suzushii** = is cool, is cold

▪ NOTES ▪

けっこう **kekkō** is used to express a feeling that something turns out better than expected (e.g. food that is more delicious than expected). It can be translated as "quite" or "rather." Refer to Phrase 126 for the use of ね **NE** as a sentence ending.

WRITE THE FOLLOWING IN JAPANESE:

1. My friend is quite smart.

2. This restaurant is quite expensive, isn't it?

3. This summer is quite cold, isn't it?

1. 私の友だちは、けっこう頭がいいです。
2. このレストランは、けっこう高いですね。
3. 今年の夏は、けっこう涼しいですね。